Integration of the Negro in the U.S. Armed Forces

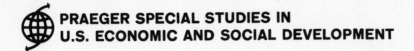

**PRAEGER SPECIAL STUDIES IN
U.S. ECONOMIC AND SOCIAL DEVELOPMENT**

Integration of the Negro in the U.S. Armed Forces

Richard J. Stillman, II

FREDERICK A. PRAEGER, Publishers
New York · Washington · London

The purpose of the Praeger Special Studies is to make specialized research monographs in U.S. and international economics and politics available to the academic, business, and government communities. For further information, write to the Special Projects Division, Frederick A. Praeger, Publishers, 111 Fourth Avenue, New York, N.Y. 10003.

FREDERICK A. PRAEGER, PUBLISHERS
111 Fourth Avenue, New York, N.Y. 10003, U.S.A.
77-79 Charlotte Street, London W.1, England

Published in the United States of America in 1968
by Frederick A. Praeger, Inc., Publishers

Library of Congress Catalog Card Number: 67-23968

Printed in the United States of America

FOR MY MOTHER
AND FATHER

PREFACE

Idealism and historicism have often hindered understanding of the relationship between the Negro and the military
arm of the United States Government. Idealistic value judgments strongly favoring one group or the other have blocked
a clear view of the political forces affecting the relationship
and have distorted its political significance. The historian's
factual approach has bogged down the student in a mass of details on troop movement, battlefield combat, and unit administration, rather than developing a broad framework for analyzing how the Negro and the armed forces interact.

This book can be criticized for avoiding the two familiar
approaches. Analysis has been emphasized at the cost of de-
tail. For some, this methodology may be too general. But
this effort develops a view of the whole Negro-military part-
nership rather than confining itself to a particular time period or organizational unit. A bibliographical essay at the
end will permit those who desire more specifics to find the
best sources for the data.

Furthermore, sympathetic criticism of both the Negro
and the military will replace value judgments favoring one
side or the other. This approach undoubtedly will irk some
of the staunch allies of either group but is essential for gaining
a clearer perspective and deeper understanding. It is hoped
that, ultimately, this political analysis will serve to better the
relationship between Negroes and the defense establishment.

CONTENTS

LIST OF TABLES AND DOCUMENTS

DOCUMENTS

Integration of the Negro in the U.S. Armed Forces

CHAPTER **1** THE POLITICAL
RELATIONSHIP OF THE
NEGRO AND THE MILITARY

The underlying premise of this book is that the Negro
and the military organization always have been interdependent,
from the smoke-filled battlefield to the smoke-filled Pentagon
conference room. The Negro has desired to share, like every
other American minority, in the patriotic, heroic, and social
rewards derived from service in the armed forces. The defense establishment has needed Negroes to fill its ranks in
every war since the Revolution; colored soldiers have participated in every war that America has fought.

What form the relationship between the Negro and the
military should take has generated considerable debate.
Ought the Negro be treated as equal to or inferior to the white
soldier? Essentially, the issue of equality--who should be
where, when, and how[1]--has created conflict between an organization devoted to warfare and preparing for it and a sociological class that our society has often deprived of the economic and social benefits taken for granted by others. Equality has been the central issue in the relationship since the
first Negroes enlisted in Washington's Continental Army for
the Battle of Bunker Hill.[2] And equality is still today an issue
when civil-rights groups protest the disproportionately high
Negro death rate in the Vietnam war.[3] Should the Negro receive the same treatment as the white? If so, how should the
Negro receive the same treatment as the white? These issues thread through the history of Negro-military relations
right into the present time.

Unfortunately, no logical answers on which everyone
can agree have emerged, and so the outcome has been largely
shaped by political forces--the passions, attitudes, and beliefs of the participants. This study will attempt to construct
a framework for understanding the basic issues in the Negro-
military relationship--all revolving around the central theme
of equality.

1

First, what major historical trends of Negro-military relations have influenced current problems? From the Revolution onward, what was the Negro's role in the American military? How did he serve, and where did he serve? What was the major reason for the development of a Jim Crow Army? Was it armed-forces policy or civilian pressure that encouraged segregation?

Second, from 1940 to 1953, by what process did the armed forces make the move from segregation to integration, a shift that occurred before the Brown Decision by the Supreme Court?[4] What was the major source of resistance to change and why? Who were the main reformers and why? What impact did integration have upon the Defense Department? Upon the Negro community? Upon the nation at large?

A third question deals with the current Negro-military relationship. What are the problems? Why do they persist? What are the best means available to the Pentagon for solving them? What solutions are likely?

Finally, there are questions related to the general political significance of what happened to this minority within the defense organization. Are there principles to be derived for determining under what political conditions human equality can best be achieved? In short, does this study of Negroes and the Defense Department offer students of effective government some abiding ideas about how different races can live with one another in greater harmony?

As a student of politics, I am interested not in value judgments or moral questions but rather in the political forces that brought about what eventually happened to Negroes in uniform. All too often this subject has been treated with either sympathy for the Negro or a pro-military attitude uppermost. While it is difficult to shake loose these prejudices, doing so permits a clearer picture of reality. But what is political analysis? How does it differ from a mere recapitulation of historic events? Or a sociological study of Negroes as soldiers? Particularly, how can political analysis be applied to further the understanding of Negro-military relations?

One dimension that this study treats is the interaction of the attitudes and goals of the two groups as a deciding factor in their relationship. The military's professional ideals, organizational policies, and expressed personal attitudes toward Negroes have inhibited or encouraged their relationship. Similarly, the Negro community's attitudes, as expressed by their leadership, protest organizations, and periodicals, have either inhibited or encouraged military participation by Negroes and, thus, weakened or strengthened the relationship. Right or wrong, these attitudes existed and profoundly influenced the decision-making processes of each side. Goals will be considered because they are important to understanding the dynamics of this association.

A second aspect of this study concerns the nature of the organization and group structure and how it affects associations between the Negro and the military. [5] How the defense establishment is organized in order to obtain its goals has influenced how it has treated the Negro. The nature of its structure, the pressures on the organization, and the peculiarities of authoritarian life have been major factors in determining whether it included or excluded colored men. On the other hand, the Negroes' sociological class structure--the numbers who are educated, who are professionally oriented, who are in leadership roles, or who are in unskilled jobs-- has influenced their inclusion or exclusion from the military. Moreover, both the military and Negro structures have been in a constant state of flux, particularly in the twentieth century. How they have been transformed by external and internal pressures has influenced the resulting pattern of race relations.

Allies and the demands of alliances are an additional pressure on the relationship between the armed forces and the Negro. Harold D. Lasswell has defined personnel in the military organization as "managers of violence. "[6] Gunnar Myrdal has characterized the plight of the Negro in the United States as "the American dilemma. "[7] Both the soldier, in his role of preparing for war, and the Negro, in his situation as second-class American citizen, have developed certain alliances with other groups in our society. Southerners have traditionally supported military designs, [8] and Negroes have been often aided by liberal-reform groups. [9]

Finally, this study will analyze intergroup political bargaining. As already described, while the Negro and military groups have needed each other in order to fulfill their ends (the Negro's desire for patriotic expression and the military's demands for troops), their conflict has centered on the distribution of Negro personnel (who should be where, when, and how). Negro power groups sought more influential assignments for their race. This jockeying for more desirable positions--who had the influence, how was it used, by what means was influence communicated, and what effects were achieved--is an important consideration in this study. Political bargaining between the military and the Negro has been rather low-keyed, due to the limitations of the political position of the two groups. The services have been restricted in their exercise of influence by the ingrained American liberal distrust of a strong military establishment.[10] The Negro minority has often found expression difficult, even impossible, because of the deep antagonism of the white majority.[11] Thus both the military and the Negro, although in very different ways, have been limited in their capability for bargaining.

But before embarking on this study, it might be reasonable to pause and ask: Why study the Negro and the military? Why not examine the Italians and the military? Or, for that matter, the whites and the military?

There are two cogent reasons for singling out the Negro. First, the most important domestic issue in America today is the position of the Negro--his economic, social, and political status. And this question has been with us ever since the first Dutch slave ship docked in Jamestown in 1619 with twenty colored persons aboard.[12] Those few Negroes were not much of a problem. But the past decade of unrest--riots in Detroit, Watts, and Harlem; school segregation in Prince George County, Maryland, and Boston; bus boycotts in Birmingham; marches on Washington; the words of James Baldwin, Richard Wright, Rap Brown, Stokely Carmichael, and Martin Luther King--reflects the discontent of these seventeenth-generation Americans at their unequal roles in a democratic nation.[13] It is hoped that this book will shed some light on their plight in one area of the American scene, the armed forces.

Second, of all areas of the United States, the military establishment has advanced the most rapidly in race relations since World War II. The armed forces in 1948 were ordered by President Truman to provide equal treatment for Negroes. By the end of the Korean conflict, the services were fully integrated. Today, Negroes comprise more than 8 per cent of the armed forces: 285,000 of them serve in every kind of job and geographic area of the defense organization. They have representation in the officer corps, holding every rank from second lieutenant to general. They comprise 20 per cent of the fighting troops in South Vietnam. [14] And as one white American company commander in South Vietnam, Captain Henry B. Tucker of the 173rd Airborne Brigade, has said: "I see only one color. And that's olive drab."[15]

But the armed services have not always been so color blind. Just twenty years ago, in World War II, 3 million Negroes registered for service and 695,264 were inducted. Of these, only 2,500 saw integrated service, and it was limited to three months in the spring of 1945, during a critical need for combat troops in Europe. The rest of the time, they served in segregated units. [16]

Some Pentagon policymakers at one time seriously considered Antarctica as a good site for training colored servicemen, [17] because it was removed from white racial fears. During the war, many colored men were embittered by their limited opportunity for combat. More than two thirds of them served in support units, such as transportation, quartermaster, and mess detachments. Until 1944, all the Navy's 165,000 Negroes were assigned to the stewards' branch ("cooks and bellhops at sea" was their nickname). [18]

What many white officers thought of Negroes was summarized in one commanding officer's advice to another white commander of a Negro unit stationed in England:[19]

> Colored soldiers are akin to well-meaning but irresponsible children... under influence such as excitement, fear, religion, dope, liquor or the accomplishment of something without their usual sphere, they individually or collectively can change form with amazing rapidity from a timid or bashful individual to brazen boldness or madness or become hysterical... The colored individual likes to "doll up," to strut, brag and show off. He likes to be distinctive and stand out from others. Everything possible should be used to encourage this. For example, know their names and occasionally call a man "Corporal John" in place of "Corporal

Smith. " In selection of NCO's, the real black
bosses should be picked rather than the lighter
"smart boy. "

Before investigating the rapid process by which the
services became integrated, let us first study how they became segregated.

CHAPTER **2** THE HISTORICAL
CONTEXT

THE UNSTABLE RELATIONSHIP

Four main historical periods are apparent in the Negro-
military relationship up to 1940: The first era was during the
Revolution, when Negroes served in integrated military units;
the second period was from after the Revolutionary War until
1863, when there were few opportunities for Negroes to enter
the Army or Navy; the third was from 1863 until the end of
the Spanish-American War, when Republican power supported
Negroes' rights to military enlistment; and the fourth period,
beginning in 1900, saw the introduction of rigid Negro segregation and job exclusion into the military.

Negroes point to their role in the American Revolution
to prove their close identity with the early national heritage.
Indeed, before development of strict slave codes, the Negro
was treated much like an indentured servant[1] and was permitted to participate freely in the Revolution. At one time or
another, 5,000 Negroes were in the colonial army and fought
in almost every engagement, north and south, on land or sea.
Since few owned land or wealth, none served as officers, but
several became legendary heroes--Attucks, Whipple, Salem,
Poor. Most served as common foot soldiers.[2]

Washington's headquarters did make an early attempt to
exclude Negroes from the Army. In 1775, several policy
directives--July 9, September 26, October 8, and November
12--prevented Negro enlistments. These orders were issued
mainly because southern slaveholding interests claimed that
they were necessary to prevent their property from disappear-
ing into the Army.[3] However, these attempts to exclude Negroes from the Army were quickly repealed by the Continental
Congress on January 16, 1776, at Washington's request.

7

Three factors prompted this reversal: First, the free Negroes in Washington's Army, many of whom had served since Bunker Hill, bitterly protested to their commander that they were being rejected after faithful service. [4] Second, the Continentals found themselves bidding against the British for Negro fighting men. In November, the British Governor of Virginia, Lord Dunmore, organized 300 slaves into a regiment to suppress the rebellious colonists. [5] Although they were never used effectively in combat and were disbanded by June, the Americans became alarmed at the possibility that all the blacks, who comprised nearly half the population of many Southern colonies, would hasten to the side of the Crown if they were barred from the colonial forces. Though the colonials hastily changed their policy, some 14,000 Negroes joined the British side, and many of them subsequently gained their liberty in the West Indies. [6] Third, as manpower shrank, the colonies were increasingly willing to take any volunteer, particularly since they had promised the Congress that they would keep their militias at a certain strength. In fact, several colonies offered Negroes both freedom and pay for enlisting. Only Georgia and South Carolina refused to allow Negroes to enter their militias. [7] In only three colonies--Connecticut, Rhode Island, and Massachusetts--were all-Negro units formed. All such units were small, short-lived, and participated in few engagements. [8] Essentially, during the Revolution, Negroes fought side by side with whites, participating in most battles, and producing about the same number of heroes for the American and the British causes.

From 1783 until 1860, the South developed its rigid institution of slavery and the North separated colored from white society. [9] Political pressures were instituted to deny Negroes the honor and prestige derived from military service, based on the common attitude that they were inferior to the high caliber of fighting men. In 1792, Congress barred Negroes from joining state militias, and in 1798 the first Secretary of the Navy, Benjamin Stoddert, prohibited Negroes and mulattoes from entering the Navy or Marines. Despite this, several hundred of them served in the naval war with France, from 1798 until 1800. [10] The War of 1812 saw two instances of Negroes in combat: A hundred were used to build and man Oliver H. Perry's ships on the Great Lakes, and General Andrew Jackson hurriedly drafted 500 New Orleans colored

men to stop Major General Edward Pakenham's advance on
the city. Contrary to the 1792 law, New York organized two
regiments of Negro troops; however, none saw action. [11]

When the war ended, so did the desire of many Americans to see Negroes in the Army or Navy. Negroes were
called on to relieve shortages of white manpower in critical
war periods, but it was not envisioned that they would con-
stitute a permanent part of the armed forces. Attorney General William Wirt in 1823 said that "it was not the intention
of Congress to incorporate Negroes and people of color with
the Army any more than with the militia."[12] Southerners
were especially outspoken. Senator John C. Calhoun in 1842
moved to exclude Negroes from the Navy except as cooks,
stewards, and servants, stating: "It was wrong to bring those
who have sustained the honor and glory of the country down to
a footing of the Negro race--to be degraded by being mingled
and mixed up with that inferior race."[13] His bill passed the
Senate but was defeated in the House. Only a handful of Negroes participated in the Mexican War, and from then until
1860, the country's professional peacetime Army and Navy
were all white, Negroes not being accepted for service.

Lincoln's policy toward Negroes in military service was
subordinate to the overriding political end of maintaining the
Union. At the beginning of the Civil War, he refrained from
using Negroes for fear of increasing hostility in the South and
driving the border states out of the Union.[14] When Lincoln
issued his first call for 75,000 volunteers, a large number of
Negroes in urban centers of the North responded with enthusiasm. In response, Secretary of War Cameron declared:
"I have to say this Department has no intention to call into
service any colored soldiers."[15] At Fort Monroe, Union General B. F. Butler offered his troops to the Governor of Maryland to put down a possible slave revolt. Thus, in 1861 there
was a shortage of men, and a few Negroes were put in uniform. However, the influx of fugitive slaves into Northern
camps prompted many field commanders to utilize them either
as informers on enemy positions or in labor gangs for construction of fortification.

In 1862, individual generals commanding three areas--
Port Royal, South Carolina; New Orleans; and Bates County,
Missouri--hard-pressed for men and situated near sympa-
thetic blacks, recruited them and formed them into separate

units to protect the military positions. The War Department did not approve, but only at Port Royal was the commander forced to disband his colored units. [16]

The Emancipation Proclamation, issued on January 1, 1863, ended Union attempts to assuage the South by with-holding Negroes from troop duty and permitted states to raise colored units. Negroes joined readily, and Union military leaders were eager to use the extra manpower. Eventually, 163 colored federal regiments and two state regiments were formed, which consisted of 178,985 men. Negroes in these units participated in 449 engagements and suffered 36,847 casualties. In addition, 250,000 served as common laborers. Few Negro soldiers were in mixed units, and most colored regiments were officered by whites. A total of 7,122 Negroes were commissioned as officers, mainly doctors and chap-lains. The expansion of the Navy, from 76 vessels in 1861 to 671 in 1865, created a persistent shortage of manpower, and by the war's end, in many craft, one-quarter of the crew were Negroes, serving on an integrated basis. [17]

In 1860, three-quarters of the nation's 4,441,830 Ne-groes lived in the South, representing a third of the Confed-eracy's population. Although Jefferson Davis strongly cen-sured Lincoln's announcement that he would use Negro sol-diers, from 1863 on there was considerable discussion in the South of using slaves in battle. However, the idea of putting slaves in uniform was too sharp a contradiction of the Con-federate conviction of Negro inferiority. But by March 15, 1865, the desperate Confederate Congress passed a last-ditch law allowing Negro enlistment. Days later, on April 2, Lee surrendered, and so no Negroes were inducted in the Southern army. [18] However, the slaves had provided invaluable logis-tical support for the South's field armies.

Thus, in both South and North the military use of Ne-groes in the Civil War was shaped by the political goals of the society--in the Union, the preservation of the nation; in the South, the defense of the belief in Negro inferiority.

After the war, on July 28, 1866, the Republicans, in an attempt to gain Negro support, established a legal require-ment that the United States Army include six units consisting of 12,500 colored veterans--the 9th and 10th Cavalry, and the 38th, 39th, 40th, and 41st Infantry. [19] A shortage of defense funds later reduced the infantry units to two--the 24th and 25th regiments. These four units, established to maintain the Negro's right to a position in the military, were primarily concerned with Indian fighting. The 9th Cavalry was stationed at the Department of the Platte in the Dakotas; the 10th at Assiniboine, Montana; the 24th Infantry at Fort Douglas, close to Salt Lake City; and the 25th at Missoula, Montana. For exceptional heroism in fighting various tribes, Negro soldiers were awarded twenty Medals of Honor by Congress.[20]

Because of a need for trained officers and because of the election in the Reconstructed South of several colored Representatives, who could appoint candidates to the academy, West Point during the 1870s opened its doors to Negroes. James W. Smith, from South Carolina, was the first Negro admitted in 1870. He did not graduate, but three others did in the nineteenth century--Henry O. Flipper, Georgia (1877); John H. Alexander, Arkansas (1887); and Charles D. Young, Ohio (1889). Three Negroes entered Annapolis--James H. Conyers, South Carolina (1872); Alonzo G. McClellan, South Carolina (1873); and Henry E. Baker, Mississippi (1874).[21] None graduated.

Republican Governors controlled the Southern states from 1865 until 1876, aided in part by colored militia. These Negroes were trained and armed to protect Republican power. Particularly in Louisiana, Florida, and Tennessee, they were engaged in counterinsurgency combat against rebel bands of the Klu Klux Klan and White Citizen Leagues. With the fall of carpetbag government, these Negro units were disbanded.[22]

During this period, Negroes served in the United States Navy, though most often in the lowest ranks. Thirty Negro sailors were aboard the battleship Maine when it was blown up on February 15, 1898, in Havana harbor. When war was declared against Spain in April, the four Negro Army units were transferred to training centers in Texas and then Florida. Negro leaders urged Congress to establish more units for Negro volunteers who wanted to enter combat. Four federal and eight state regiments were formed, plus several smaller units, such as Company L of the 6th Massachusetts Infantry, the only Negro unit to fight as part of a white regiment. Because of a shortage of officers, the President authorized the commissioning of 100 Negro second lieutenants. The regular Negro units got to Cuba first and participated in most of the combat at El Caney, Las Guasimas, and San Juan Hill. The 9th and 10th Cavalry won considerable distinction as part of Theodore Roosevelt's Rough Riders. The Regulars and the volunteers had occupational duty in Cuba and the Philippines at the close of the Spanish-American War. [23]

At the turn of the century, the Negro was further sub-ordinated by the rise of radical Populist elements, which gained control in many sections of the country. [24] By using the Negroes (a defenseless minority) as a symbol of political corruption and social ills, they spread anti-Negro violence and encouraged rigid racial separation. The Federal Government, both executive and judicial branches, encouraged these elements by acquiescing to their demands. For example, the Supreme Court handed down the Plessy Decision, which established the separate-but-equal doctrine. [25]

The Negro-military relationship amid the social turmoil is illustrated by the Brownsville incident. In August, 1906, a riot occurred in Brownsville, Texas, on the Mexican border, where the 25th Infantry was stationed. [26] Three of its companies were involved in the riot, which killed one citizen, wounded another, and injured a police chief. Whites claimed that the Negroes had "shot up the town," although the outbreak had been provoked when a white officer fired into the crowd and mostly Negro homes had been burned. President Theodore Roosevelt, taking the word of one inspector who said the Negroes had murdered and maimed citizens of the town, dismissed all three companies, without a fair inquiry. Negroes were angered at the rash action. Three years later, their protests and the efforts of Ohio Senator Foraker resulted in a court of inquiry, which cleared the discharged men and restored their rank and back pay. Despite this vindication, the riot had a lasting effect upon the military's view of the Negro's discipline and character, which it thereafter judged to be questionable.

World War I brought a further decline in Negro-military relations. Under Selective Service, 3 million Negroes were registered and 350,000 were inducted, but the conditions that confronted them in the military were humiliating. Unfortunately, the Wilson Administration was largely dependent upon Southern Democratic power. In order to maintain his Southern support, the President had to ignore what was happening to the Negro in the military, as well as elsewhere in the Federal

Government and in the nation as a whole.[27] Moreover, Secretary of War Newton Baker appointed as his aides on racial
matters Emmett Scott and later Robert Moton. Both men had
worked under Booker T. Washington and held his view on the
importance of social inactivism for the Negro, a philosophy
that Washington had explained at the Cotton States and International Exposition in Atlanta in 1895:

> The wisest among my race understand that the
> agitation of questions of social equality is the ex-
> tremest folly, and that progress in the enjoyment
> of all privileges that will come to us must be the
> result of severe and constant struggles rather than
> of artificial forcing.[28]

Moreover, the Negroes' relationship with the military
was exacerbated by the situation within the Army and Navy.

A basic problem for the Negro soldiers was the geographic position of bases. Large Negro units were stationed
in Manhattanville, Kansas; Houston, Texas; and Spartansburg,
South Carolina. The citizens of these neighboring communities were inhospitable to these troops and on occasion provoked riots when the men entered their towns.[29] The services, organizing for wartime, disliked the added problems
that thus accompanied the training of colored troops. They
tried to keep Negroes on the military post, away from possible tension. Brigadier General Charles C. Ballou, commander of the 92nd Negro Division at Camp Funston, Kansas,
warned his 27,000 Negro troops not to begin racial conflicts:

> To avoid such conflicts the Division Commander
> has repeatedly urged all colored members of his
> command and especially officers and noncommis-
> sioned officers to refrain from going where his
> presence will be resented.

> ... good will depends on the public. The public
> is nine-tenths white. White men made the Division
> and they can break it just as easy if it becomes a
> troublemaker.[30]

This policy of isolation was carried overseas in an
American command memo, "Secret Information Concerning
Black American Troops," issued to French leaders on

August 7, 1918:

>Although a citizen of the United States, the black
>man is regarded by the white American as an in-
>ferior being with whom relations of business or
>service only are possible.... .
>
>We must prevent the rise of any pronounced
>degree of intimacy between French officers and
>black officers.... .
>
>We must not commend too highly the black
>American troops, particularly in the presence of
>white Americans.... .
>
>Make a point of keeping the native population
>from spoiling the Negroes. White Americans be-
>come incensed at any public expression of intimacy
>between white women and black men.... .[31]

The French did not pay much attention to the "Secret
Information," but its publication in Negro periodicals made
colored persons sharply hostile toward Army leaders. Thus,
the military's effort to avoid tension succeeded only in
creating it.

Dissatisfaction with this attitude was reflected in the
questions published in one Negro journal:[32]

>Emmett Scott, did you know the treatment which
>black troops were receiving in France?
>If you did not know, why did you not find out?
>If you did know, what did you do about it?

Second, the method of military groupment, the require-
ment to rigidly segregate troops, forced the services to develop division-size Negro units (the 92nd and 93rd Infantry
divisions). The 93rd Division, made up primarily of National
Guard volunteer regiments, arrived in France in May, 1917,
where it was immediately broken up. Each of its four regiments (369th, 370th, 371st, and 372nd) fought with a French
division in various parts of the line.[33] All received considerable recognition from French and American authorities for
their combat record. The 157th French Division commander,
General Gobyet, praised the exploits of the 371st and 372nd:

The 157th French Division will never forget the
wonderful irresistible impetus, the heroic rush
of the colored American regiments on the "Observa-
tories Crest" and on the Plain of Menthois.   The
most formidable defense, the nests of machine guns,
the best-organized position, the most crushing artillery barrages could not stop them. [34]

The 92nd, primarily made up of draftees, arrived in
France in June, 1917, and was maintained as a whole division.
Its effectiveness was impaired by inadequate training for
battle and high racial tension between its white officers and
Negro soldiers.   Charles Houston, a Negro lieutenant in the
368th Regiment of the 92nd Division, and later to be dean of
the Howard University Law School, stated:

> The hate and scorn heaped upon us as Negro offi-
> cers by Americans, at Camp Mencou and Vannes,
> in France, convinced me there was no sense in
> dying in a world ruled by them.... They boarded us
> off from our fellow white officers.   They made us
> eat on benches in order to maintain segregation,
> and they destroyed our prestige in front of French
> officers. [35]

The Washingtonian philosophy is evident in the speeches
of Robert R. Moton, a former aide of Booker T. Washington
at Tuskegee Institute.   Moton was asked by President Wilson
to go to France on December 2, 1918, and explain to the Negro troops that they must return to America without causing
disturbances.   In a speech he gave to the 92nd Division, Moton
said:

> You will go back to America heroes, as you really
> are.   You will go back as you have carried your-
> selves over here--in a straightforward, manly, and
> modest way.   If I were you, I would find a job as
> soon as possible and get to work.   To those who have
> not already done so, I would suggest that you get
> hold of a piece of land and a home as soon as pos-
> sible and marry and settle down... Save your money,
> and put it into something tangible.   I hope no one
> will do anything in peace to spoil the magnificent
> record you have made in war. [36]

Another source of trouble was the large military need for support units. World War I required mass armies but had a lower automated capability than today for supporting the military. [37] Colored men largely filled the noncombat roles. Of 213 port battalions, 106 consisted of Negroes. Negroes comprised one tenth of the population, one eighth of the armed forces, one thirtieth of the combat strength, but one third of the military labor force. [38]

Finally, tensions arose over the inadequate number and quality of Negro officers. The last Negro had graduated from West Point in 1889. [39] While several had entered during the Spanish-American War and through Reserve training, only a handful of Negro officers were on duty at the beginning of World War I. This aroused considerable Negro protest, and a training school for Negroes was established in Des Moines, which eventually commissioned 1,408 officers (.07 per cent of the 200,000 officers serving in World War I). [40] But these were too few, too poorly trained, and commissioned too late to alleviate the chronic deficiency in leadership. Furthermore, many Negroes were disappointed because the senior colored officer, Colonel Charles D. Young, retired before the war due to high blood pressure, never got an opportunity to lead Negro troops. [41]

The Navy had never commissioned any Negro officers, and the Roosevelt Administration had restricted Negroes to the steward branch. Ten thousand Negroes served in the Navy as messmen and cooks during World War I. None were admitted into the Marines. [42]

The poor treatment of the colored in World War I engendered deep bitterness in the Negro community. Conversely, their consignment to supportive functions, the poor military record of the 92nd Division, and the problems of racial tension caused the soldiering profession to distrust the Negro capability for combat duty.

A good indication of the military attitude that was to prevail for nearly the next thirty years is found in a letter that Colonel Allen J. Greer, chief of staff of the 92nd Division, wrote to Senator Kenneth D. McKallor of Ohio on December 6, 1918:

We came to France in June, were given seven
weeks in training instead of four weeks in training
area usually allotted.   From there we went to the
Argonne and the offensive starting there on September 26, had one regiment in the line.   They
failed in all their missions, laid down and sneaked
to the rear, until they were withdrawn.   Thirty
of the officers of this regiment alone were reported
either for cowardice or failure to prevent their men
from retreating--and this was against very little
opposition.

During our career, counting the time in America,
we have had about 30 cases of rape, among which
was one where 22 men at Camp Grant raped one
woman, and we have had 8, I believe, reported in
France with about 15 attempts besides.

During the entire time we have been operating,
there has never been a single operation conducted
by a colored officer, where his report did not have
to be investigated by a field officer to find out what
the real facts were.   Accuracy and ability to de-
scribe facts is lacking in all, and most of them are
just plain liars in addition. [43]

William E. DuBois, editor of Crisis Magazine and the
first Negro to obtain a Ph. D. in history from Harvard, went
to France and spent several months talking with soldiers.   His
remarks, printed in June, 1919, reflect the Negroes' pro-
found resentment toward the Army.

About the white officers, he said:

It seemed that instead of trying to increase morale
of his division, it was General Ballou's [the 92nd
Division commander] intention to discourage the
men as much as possible.   His action in censuring
officers in the presence of enlisted men was an act
that tended toward breaking down the confidence
that the men had in their officers, and he pursued
this method on innumerable occasions.   On one
occasion he referred to his division, in talking to

another officer, as the "rapist division"; he constantly cast aspersions on the work of the colored officers and permitted other officers to do the same in his presence. [44]

DuBois pointed to the excellent record of the 369th Regiment in the 93rd Division as proof of the Negro's combat ability:

In all, the 369th was under fire 191 days--a record for any American unit. It received over 170 citations for the Croix de Guerre and Distinguished Service Cross and was the first unit of the Allied armies to reach the Rhine, November 18, with the 2nd French Army. [45]

He emphasized the poor officer instruction and treatment:

At the colored officer-training camp, no instruction was given in artillery and a deadline was established by which no one was commissioned higher than captain, despite several recommendations.

The world which General Ballou and his field officers tried to re-create for Negro officers was a world of continuous daily insult and discrimination to the extent that none has ever experienced. [46]

DuBois discussed the problem of rape:

On one subject the white commanding officers of all colored units showed more solicitude than on the organization and fighting efficiency of the troops--that was the relations of colored officers and men with women of France. They began by officially stigmatizing the Negroes as rapists; they solemnly warned the troops in speeches and general order not even to speak to women on the street; ordered the whites' military police to spy on blacks and arrest them if they found them talking with French women. The white troops, taking their cue from all this senseless pother, spread tales and rumors among peasants and villagers and sought to chastise Negroes and offending

women. One officer, a high-minded gentleman,
graduate and Phi Beta Kappa man of a leading
American institution, was courtmartialed for
keeping company with a perfectly respectable
girl...

While the 92nd Division was in France, there
were 14 trials for attacks on women, six of which
were acquitted, of the eight others, one man has
been found guilty and hanged. No other American
division in France has a better record. [47]

Was Greer or DuBois correct? Certainly, both were
honest in their views. DuBois was nearer the truth in that the
92nd's incidence of rape did not differ much from that of other
American units, that Negro soldiers did receive considerable
heaps of scorn from the 92nd's white officers, and that the
individual Negro regiments of the 93rd serving in the French
line had a good record and received better treatment from
French officers. But Greer, a professional soldier whose
task was to prepare and lead men into battle, was correct in
that the 92nd took longer to train, was harder to control, and
did worse in battle than other American units. But this was
not the fault of the Negroes who served in the 92nd. Rather,
the soldiering profession had created the problem. Because
of rigid segregation, the promotion of few Negro officers,
white leadership, training in Southern communities, and few
recreational opportunities, the Negroes of the 92nd ended up
fighting their white commanders harder than their German
enemy, and thus were a weak unit.

The armed forces, when they returned to a small peace-
keeping constabulary in the 1920's and 1930's, reduced Negro
units to minimal strength and for several years abolished
Negro recruitment. [48] In his autobiography, General Robert
Lee Bullard, commander of the 2nd Army, of which the 92nd
Division was a part, warned the Army of the dangers of using
Negroes and the need for strict separation in order to main-
tain military effectiveness. [49] A War College report, "Use of
Negro Manpower" (November 12, 1936), reflected the mili-
tary's view of Negroes:

As an individual, the Negro is docile, tractable,
lighthearted, carefree, and good-natured. If
unjustly treated, he is likely to become surly and

> stubborn, though this is a temporary phase. He
> is careless, shiftless, irresponsible and secretive.
> He resents censure and is best handled with praise
> and ridicule. He is unmoral, untruthful, and his
> sense of right doing is relatively inferior. Crimes
> and convictions involving moral turpitude are
> nearly five to one compared with convictions of
> whites on similar charges.... Their emotions are
> unstable and their reactions uncertain. Bad
> leadership in particular is easily communicated
> to them. [50]

The military profession--the Greers, Ballous and Bullards--ignored the excellent record of the 93rd Division. But Secretary of War Newton D. Baker was aware of it when he wrote:

> The circumstances disclosed by a detailed study
> of the situation did not justify many of the highly
> colored accounts which have been given of the
> behavior of the troops in this action, and they
> afford no basis at all for any of the general as-
> sumptions with regard to the action of the colored
> troops in the battle and elsewhere in France. On
> the contrary, it is to be noted that many colored
> officers and particularly three in the very battalion
> here under discussion were decorated with Dis-
> tinguished Service Crosses for extraordinary
> heroism under fire. [51]

Nonetheless, the Republican statute adopted in 1866 in order to secure the Negro's right to military service in four colored units was used in the early twentieth century by the soldiering profession to segregate the Negro and thus sup- posedly protect military efficiency. Unfortunately, this mili- tary philosophy of Jim Crow carried into World War II, pro- voking harsh reactions by Negroes and thereby increasing the very thing that the armed forces were trying so hard to pre- vent--inefficiency on the battlefield.

SUMMARY

From the Revolutionary War until 1940, the relationship between the Negro and the military had been inconsistent. When the military needed men, Negroes served. When it did

not, Negroes were rejected. When the Republicans sought
their support in 1866, colored units were established and the
doors at West Point and Annapolis swung open for Negroes.
When the Southerners regained a strong political position in
the early 19th and 20th centuries, Negroes were rejected.

The Negroes had not been lacking in enthusiasm to don
the uniform and participate in America's wars, but they had
been enormously lacking in the ability to assert their political
rights to serve in the armed forces. The Negro fought on the
battlefield but could not fight in the political arena, where his
military role was ultimately determined. He was not repre-
sented when his military destiny was decided because large
obstacles--slavery, legalized inequality, ineffective Negro
leadership--blocked him from making demands for government
action.

CHAPTER 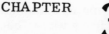 THE MOVEMENT FROM
SEGREGATION TO
INTEGRATION, 1940-53

THE EXPERIENCE OF WORLD WAR II

The role of the Negro in World War II was decided by
World War I. The military, because of its preoccupation with
the record of the 92nd Division and disregard of the exploits
of the regiments of the 93rd, had a low opinion of Negroes'
abilities. This attitude was well reflected in a 1940 Army War
College study, which described them as having "less developed
mental capacities."[1] On the other hand, Negroes were not
keen on serving in an Army that did not want them. By 1940,
only five officers and 5,000 enlisted men were left in the all-
Negro units, which had numbered 100,000 in the prewar Army.
Only two of the five officers were in combat branches, and
they were father and son, Benjamin O. Davis, Sr. and Jr. The
Navy Department had even poorer relations with Negroes; it
accepted them only as stewards. The Marines accepted no
Negroes.

The military, incapable of thinking about alternatives to
racial segregation, undertook to use again in World War II the
system that had generated such bad feeling in World War I. Between the wars, the Negroes had not given much thought to the
situation other than to condemn the armed forces. Even if they
had wanted to voice dissent, they had mobilized few political
means of expressing their views; in 1940, only one colored
Congressman was elected, from Chicago.[2]

The old system used by the armed forces had these
characteristics:

First, it excluded Negroes from many jobs in the services. Negroes were not allowed at all in the Marines. In
1941, all 5,026 Negroes in the Navy were in the stewards'
branch. By 1943, nineteen Negro Navy Seabee (Construction

Battalion) units (18, 600 men) were building port facilities and
coast defenses, but except for stewards, no other Navy jobs
were open to Negroes.   The Army was unwilling to teach Negroes certain skills.   Despite the rapid growth in importance
of air power at the beginning of World War II, the Army Air
Corps was closed to colored volunteers. [3]

Second, large segregated units were organized.   An all-
colored 2nd Cavalry Division was formed at Fort Clark,
Texas, in February, 1943.   The 92nd Division of World War I
was reactivated in October, 1942, at Fort Hauchuca, Arizona,
with 12, 000 men and 500 Negro officers making up the 365th,
370th, and 371st Infantry regiments and 597th, 598th, and
600th Field Artillery battalions.   Also, the 93rd Division was
reactivated in May, 1942, at Camp Clipper, California, with
the 368th, and 369th Infantry regiments and the 593rd, 595th,
and 596th Field Artillery battalions.   Because of Negro demands, an all-colored 99th Fighter Squadron was activated October 2, 1942, and in Italy in 1943 was expanded to the 332nd
Fighter Group.

In 1942, the Navy set up separate training facilities for
Negroes.   A basic-training camp was established at the Great
Lakes Training Center in Illinois, and a vocational-training
station was set up at Hampton Institute in Virginia.   Segregation applied to off-duty hours, too.   NCO clubs, officer clubs,
and USO facilities were separate.   The Red Cross even established a Jim Crow blood bank, although a Negro physician,
Dr. Charles R. Drew, was responsible, along with Dr. John
Scudder, for developing blood plasma. [4]

Third, the Negro's role was primarily in support rather
than combat.   (See Table 1.)   The Army assigned one out of
five Negroes to the engineers responsible for manual labor,
which built such facilities as the Alcan military highway, the
Anzio Beach port, landing fields in England, and the Ledo
Road from India to China.   In port units 77 per cent of the men
were Negroes, and these Negro port units were responsible
for loading and unloading 20 million tons of war materials.   In
transportation, 69 per cent of the servicemen were Negro.
More than three fourths of the Red Ball express, which sup-
plied the Allied drive on Germany in 1944, was staffed by Negro drivers.   A third of chemical troops, 22 per cent of sig-
nal units, and 11 per cent of ordnance units were Negro. [5]

TABLE 1

Occupational Distribution of Uniformed Negro and White Personnel in World War II
(January 1, 1943)

Unit Type	Whites	Negroes	Percentage of Negroes	Distribution by % of Race Throughout Military	
				White	Negro
Combat	1,815,094	92,772	4.8	40.0	19.7
Service	616,851	161,707	20.7	13.6	34.6
Army Air Force	1,190,363	109,637	8.4	26.4	23.5
Overheads (hospital and administrative)	303,820	65,880	15.3	8.0	14.1
RTC (Officer Training)	238,500	27,500	10.3	5.3	5.9
OCS (Officer Training)	72,000	800	1.1	1.5	0.2
Unassigned	235,289	9,587	3.9	5.2	2.1

Source: Ulysses Lee, The Employment of Negro Troops World War II (Unpublished, 1966).

24

Even the Negroes in combat divisions spent little time fighting and much time in reserve. The 93rd was restricted to housekeeping and mopping-up exercises in the South Pacific, and throughout the war served as support for the Eighth Army. According to General Douglas MacArthur, "lack of ships prevented us from moving the 93rd to forward areas."[6] The 2nd Cavalry Division, though trained in the United States as a combat division, was broken up into service units (engineer, port, transportation battalions) as soon as it arrived in Africa because of the pressing military demand for these support organizations.

Walter White, national secretary of the NAACP, who was in Europe inspecting Negro troops at the time the 2nd Cavalry was reorganized from combat to support units, describes the scene:

> I was taken to a hillside from whose natural amphitheater one looked out upon the blue expanse of the Mediterranean. At the foot of the hill was a microphone to which I was escorted. Seated on the hillside were between five and six thousand Negro soldiers. The late afternoon sun lighted up the thousands of battle helmets. An ominous brooding, intent silence hung like a pall over them. Little applause, even of the courtesy variety, followed my introduction. The unit had been trained for combat and shipped overseas a few weeks before I encountered them in Oran. But they had arrived in North Africa at the time when port battalions were needed to unload ships. Though there were many Italian prisoners of war available for such manual labor and a large number of American soldiers who had been inactive at Oran for some time, who might have served as port battalions, the decision had been made to transform this outfit from combat to service status. The sudden transition had driven morale to the vanishing point. No speech I have ever made before or since was more difficult than the feeble and ineffective one on that occasion. I could only assure them that I knew the reasons for their dejection and that those of us who were in a position to, would do all we could.[7]

But this is not to say that Negroes never saw combat.
The 99th Fighter Squadron (later the 332nd Fighter Group)
arrived in North Africa in April, 1943, and in the year following, flew 800 sorties and participated in air battles over
Anzio Beach, Sicily, and Pantelleria, Italy. By V-E Day, the
unit had flown 1,579 missions, 15,533 sorties, received 865
awards, and produced air heroes that included Benjamin O.
Davis, Jr., Jack D. Holdsclaw, George S. Roberts, and
Clarence D. Lester. The 92nd Division, although it did not
arrive in Italy until August, 1944, fought as part of General
Mark Clark's Fifth Army, taking heavy losses while crossing
the Arno River, occupying the Lucca Canal, and engaging in
mountain combat in northern Italy. In battle, it sustained
25 per cent casualties, received 12,098 military decorations,
and produced such combat heroes as Kenneth W. Coleman,
John W. Madison, Reuben Horner, Vernon J. Baker, and
Charles F. Gandy. [8] Even though restricted to the Navy stewards' branch, Negro sailors showed a capability for combat.
Three won the Navy Cross for extraordinary heroism in
battle--Dorie Miller, aboard the USS Arizona at Pearl Harbor;
Leonard Roy Harmon on the USS San Francisco in the Solomons;
and William Pinckney, at sea on the USS Enterprise. [9]

Fourth, Negroes were underrepresented in leadership
posts of the Defense Department. Midway through the war,
Benjamin O. Davis, Sr., was promoted to brigadier general--
the first Negro general--but his role was primarily that of
racial adviser to the European Command. Similarly, three
Negroes served as Pentagon civil-rights counselors--William
Hastie for the Army Air Corps, Truman Gibson for the War
Department, and Lester Granger for the Navy Department.
However, none held command or leadership posts. Perhaps
their single most tangible achievement was William Hastie's
resignation from his post, deploring the Army's foot-dragging
acceptance of Negro flyers, on January 30, 1943. He was a
determined enemy of the segregation practiced by the military:

> ...there are millions of Americans outside of the
> Armed Services...who will never cease fighting
> to remove all racial barriers and every humiliating
> practice which now confronts us. [10]

His well-publicized disagreement with the Army Air Corps and
the publication of his "On Clipped Wings" forced the military
to do more for colored flyers by organizing the 99th Fighter

Squadron. [11] Better representation inside the Pentagon was
probably hindered most by the political weakness of the Negro
community outside. In 1944, there were only two Negro Congressmen, ineffective Negro protest organizations, and few
colored publications. [12]

This discriminatory situation caused considerable Negro
discontent within and outside the services. Hardly a month
went by without some base having a racial disturbance because
Negroes felt they were treated unfairly by white leaders.
Open riots broke out at Army posts in Hawaii, Alexandria,
Louisiana; and Camp Stewart, Georgia. [13] The Navy also experienced racial clashes: the Port Chicago mutiny at San
Francisco, July 17, 1944; the Guam disorders, December 25,
1944; the Seabee hunger strike at Camp Rousseau, California,
March, 1945; and the Seabee discharge case of the 80th Bat-
talion, October, 1943. [14]

Despite these problems, by V-J Day, 3 million Negroes
had registered for service, 695,264 had been inducted, and
495,950 had gone overseas. Most of these servicemen had
written home about their military experiences, sowing the
seeds for widespread Negro dissatisfaction with the Defense
Department.

However, the Negroes' dissent during World War II centered on the denial of combat roles, exclusion from certain
types of jobs, and the small number of leadership positions.
Not until after World War II, did the Negroes direct their
attacks on the segregation policies of the military. When
William H. Hastie in October, 1940, proposed creation of a
volunteer integrated unit, General George C. Marshall, who
had been raised in the belief that segregation was important to
military efficiency and who was now organizing for the war,
bluntly ended discussion by replying:

> A solution of many of the issues presented by
> Judge Hastie would be tantamount to solving a
> social problem which has perplexed the American
> people throughout the history of this nation. The
> Army cannot accomplish such a solution and
> should not be charged with such an undertaking.
> The settlement of vexing racial problems cannot

be permitted to complicate the tremendous task
of the War Department and thereby jeopardize
the discipline and morale.[15]

The World War I ghosts of Generals Ballou and Bullard
and Colonel Greer stalked the War Department halls, for as
Lieutenant Colonel J.W. Boyer advised his superior, Major
General E.S. Adams, even talking about an integration proposal would be a waste of time:

> I can see no useful purpose in any officer
> dissipating his time to discuss (the idea) with
> Mr. White or anyone else. There may be some
> super tolerant people that would join a Negro
> outfit, but their numbers would be few. Other
> whites that would join a Negro outfit would be
> the same class of whites that would live in a
> Negro community. This Judge Hastie knows
> and admits, and he does nothing to cut down
> useless and persistent correspondence on the
> subject.[16]

The civilian leadership placed first emphasis upon winning the war and thus gave in to the views of admirals and
generals on racial treatment. Secretary of the Navy Frank
Knox, in a form letter reflecting the feelings of his senior
naval officers, said that "the policy of not enlisting men of
the colored race for any branch of the naval service but the
messmen branch was adopted to meet the best interests of
general ship efficiency."[17] John J. McCloy, Assistant Secretary of War, felt that winning the war had priority over
racial innovation:

> Frankly, I do not think that the basic issues of
> this war are involved in the question of whether
> Colored troops serve in segregated units or in
> mixed units, and I doubt whether you can convince
> the people of the United States that the basic
> issues of freedom are involved in such a question.
> If the United States does not win this war, the
> lot of the Negro is going to be far, far worse
> than it is today.[18]

Not all military men thought Negroes were incapable of
fighting. General George S. Patton, commander of the 3rd

Army, told the 761st Tank Battalion on October 10, 1944:

> Men, you're the first Negro tankers ever to
> fight in the American Army. I would never have
> asked for you if you weren't good. I don't care
> what color you are, so long as you go up there
> and kill those Kraut sonsabitches. [19]

Alternatives to segregation were tried in 1944 and 1945, but not because most senior Army generals or Navy admirals wanted them. Due to acute manpower needs created by the German offensive in the Battle of the Bulge, Lieutenant General John C. H. Lee, Eisenhower's Commander of Service Forces in Europe, called for 2,500 Negro volunteers to be trained to fight in white units. [20] The men assembled at Noyons, France, on January 10, 1945, for six weeks of training. Generals Patton, Bradley, Hodges and Eisenhower approved, but Eisenhower's Chief of Staff, J. Bedell Smith, insisted that approval be obtained from General George C. Marshall, Army Chief of Staff. Marshall's staff reluctantly accepted the idea, but stipulated that instead of Negroes fighting side by side with whites, they be formed into forty-eight-man platoons commanded by white officers and a few white sergeants and that the platoons be assigned to eleven combat divisions of the First and Seventh armies.

Under this arrangement, Negroes fought successfully with white units for two months, from the end of March to V-E Day. Interviewers later found that attitudes of whites toward Negroes improved during this exposure to colored men in combat. [21] While there is some question as to the validity of the sample, since all these Negroes were volunteers and thus probably showed a higher motivation for combat than the average recruit, the statistics impressed later military committees inquiring about the Negro in the Army.

Even though these 2,500 Negroes performed well with whites for two months, the Pentagon transferred most of them into segregated units for their trip back to America. Clearly, Army policy toward the Negro had not changed at the end of the war.

The bellwether for integration of the Navy was James Forrestal. Early in 1944, he succeeded Frank Knox as Secretary of the Navy. Pressed by manpower needs and supported by his aide, Lester Granger, former secretary of the National Urban League, Forrestal reformed the Navy Department's racial policy. A 1944 "Guide to the Command of Negro Naval Personnel" reflected the changed attitude: "The Navy accepts no theories of racial differences in inborn ability, but expects that every man wearing its uniform be trained and used in accordance with his maximum individual abilities. "[22]

Soon the new attitude was translated into action. In July, 1944, the Navy abandoned its segregated advanced-training facilities for Negroes. Early in 1945, basic training was integrated. In August, 1944, the Navy organized 25 auxiliary ships (oilers, tankers, and cargo vessels) manned by crews that were 10 per cent Negro. In October, 1944, the WAVES permitted Negroes to serve as officers and enlisted personnel. In March, 1944, twelve Negro officers (two chaplains, three medics, two dentists, three supply officers, and two civil engineers) and one warrant officer graduated from the Great Lakes Training Station. They were the first of 58 Negro Naval officers to be commissioned during World War II. The Marines at last opened their ranks to 16,900 enlisted Negroes, who served until the end of the war in segregated supply and ammunition units. [23]

Despite these reforms, by V-J Day, the position of the Negro in the Navy had not significantly changed. He was still excluded from most jobs, segregated in a support role, and underrepresented in leadership positions. In September, 1945, more than 85 per cent of 165,000 Navy Negroes were in the stewards' branch.

How did World War II military policy toward the Negroes compare with that toward other racial minorities? The American-born Japanese offers a good comparison. In June, 1943, through the efforts of General John L. DeWitt, Commander of Western Defenses, and Earl Warren, then Attorney General of California, the Japanese in California were moved to sixteen assembly centers at race tracks and fairgrounds because of fears they would collaborate with the enemy. Early in 1943, the government, because of manpower needs, permitted Nisei who signed loyalty pledges to join the Army. The 442nd Regimental Combat Team was organized, consisting of 5,000 Japanese-Americans, and assigned to fight as part of General Mark W. Clark's Fifth Army in Italy.

The Nisei, no matter where he went, was considered an equal citizen. The colored citizen, even if he had a Ph. D., was judged to be inferior. A former member of the 442nd, now Senator Daniel K. Inouye, illustrates this distinction:

> During our training we were advised by our commanding officer that, according to the official ruling of some of the officials in Mississippi, while we were there in Mississippi, training, we would be considered as white people. Therefore, we were told not to enter through doors that said "Colored," not to go to colored restaurants, to go through the white entrance, to go to theatres, or sit in the front of the bus. It was a rather comical situation. Here we were, colored--because we weren't white but yet in Mississippi all of a sudden we became white folks. [24]

Moreover, the Nisei 442nd, unlike the Negro units, had a compelling motive to do well--in order to prove their patriotism and obtain freedom for their families held in American compounds. Their regimental motto was "Go for Broke," and as General Clark wrote:

> I had with my Fifth Army in Italy many nationalities, sixteen, I believe. And I took with me 5,000 Japanese-Americans, referred to as the Nisei. General Marshall had given me instructions that as soon as I put them into combat to give him an immediate report on their capacity for fighting, their loyalty and all about it. Their first battle soon took place after we landed at Salerno. And I was utterly amazed at their fighting capacity. They were valorous; they were willing to give their lives readily. And I gave a glowing report to General Marshall, and said, "If you've got any more, send them to me."[25]

The 442nd was perhaps the most decorated regiment in the American Army, and its reputation for heroism was one reason why 36,000 Japanese internees in California could go back to their homes in 1944.

DISSENT DURING THE IMMEDIATE
POSTWAR PERIOD, 1945-48

A new mood gripped America after World War II. After
fighting oppression abroad, whites and blacks turned their
eyes toward civil-rights problems in their own nation. As
Professor Robert McCloskey has written:

> ...the spectacle of the police state in Germany
> and Russia and elsewhere caused many Americans
> to revere freedom of expression more con-
> sciously than they had in the past and to resist
> attempts to inhibit it. The racist doctrines of
> Adolf Hitler and the frightful implementation
> of those doctrines in Nazi policy, helped pro-
> voke a feeling of dissatisfaction and guilt over
> America's own patterns of race discrimination.
> The right of fair trial, once taken for granted,
> assumed new layers of significance in the minds
> of men repelled by the totalitarian image. For
> some, the concern for the civil rights issue was
> enhanced by awareness that America had become
> willy-nilly the leader of the free world and must
> set a responsible leader's example. [26]

One of the first institutions to come under scrutiny was
the defense organization. The awakening queries of Pentagon
racial policies were reflected in A Study of the Negro in Military Service, written by a young white woman, Jean Byers, in
June, 1947:

> Why? Why, when the United States was making
> feverish efforts to defend its institutions and
> ways of life from Nazi aggression, did it refuse
> the support of one-tenth of its citizens? Why,
> when our nation was eager for patriots, was the
> Negro denied the right of defending his native
> land? [27]

The hearts of Negroes were not silent in relating their
feelings about the war. One cannot remain unmoved by Witter
Bynner's poem, "Defeat," picturing Nazi prisoners of war
eating with white American soldiers while Negroes assigned
to guard them were not permitted at the same table:

> On a train in Texas German prisoners eat
> With white American soldiers, seat by seat,
> While black American soldiers sit apart
> The white men eating meat, the black men heart.
> Now, with that other war a century done,
> Not the live North but the dead South has won,
> Not yet a riven nation comes awake.
> Whom are we fighting this time, for God's sake?
> Mark well the token of the separate seat.
> It is again ourselves whom we defeat. [28]

John Oliver Killen's novel, <u>And Then We Heard The Thunder</u>, describes the transformation of a young idealistic Negro, Solly Saunders, who graduates from New York City College, enlists in the Army, and finds that it is not the Japanese that he must fight but the white man. "You ain't even a second-class citizen any more, you're a second-class soldier,"[29] he is told. Because of military mistreatment, his idealism turns to embittered cynicism and, as he related to his white mistress:

> Fairness is a thing no white man has a right to
> ask of colored. I mean, look--who's being un-
> fair to whom? Who's been unfair to my mother
> and her mother and my father and his father and
> who'll be unfair to my son and his children?
> Fairness is a word that should choke in the white
> man's throat. I'm not asking any white man to
> be fair with Solly Saunders, baby. I live with
> no such false illusions. [30]

Sammy Davis' autobiography, <u>Yes I Can,</u> describes his difficulties in military life:

> I had been drafted into the Army to fight, and I
> did. We were loaded with Southerners and
> Southwesterners who got their kicks out of
> needling me, and Jennings [his Sergeant] and
> his guys never let up. I must have had a
> knockdown, drag-out fight every two days and
> I was getting pretty good with my fists. I had
> scabs on my knuckles for the first three months
> in the Army. My nose was broken again and
> getting flatter all the time. I fought clean,
> dirty, any way I could win. They were the ones

who started the fights and I didn't owe them
any Queensberry rules. It always started the
same way: a wise guy look, a sneer--once
they knew how I'd react, they were constantly
maneuvering me into more fights. [31]

After returning from visiting Negro troops stationed in
Europe, Walter White, national secretary of the NAACP,
wrote in 1945:

A wind is rising--a wind of determination by
the have nots of the world to share the benefits of freedom and prosperity which the
haves of the earth have tried to keep ex-
clusively for themselves. [32]

A prime reason for rising Negro dissent toward military
policies was the drastic change in Negro class structure
caused by World War II. In large numbers, Negroes moved
from the agrarian South to war industries of the Northeastern
and Western cities, there finding greater affluence. Some
879,000 migrated to the Northeast, and 336,000 went to the
Pacific Coast. The Southeastern states lost 484,000, and the
Southwest 336,000. [33] Most went to cities where jobs were.
Los Angeles, for example, from 1940 to 1945 doubled its Negro population, from 75,000 to 150,000. [34] Earnings from
wartime and postwar jobs more than tripled the salary of the
average Negro (in 1939, a Negro received $460 per year, and
in 1948 he got $1,615, or he formerly earned two-fifths of a
white's wage, and in 1948 he made three-fifths). [35] Higher in-
comes, steady employment, urban living boosted many more
Negroes into the middle class, as reflected in the 1940-50 increase in Negro white-collar persons (from 6 to 10 per cent),
in doctoral graduates from Negro colleges (from 56 to 164),
in home ownership (from 20 per cent to 40 per cent), and in
life expectancy for Negro males (from 45 to 58 years). [36]
Good jobs, better education, easier living gave many more
Negroes both the desire and means to demand the things other
Americans had. And they now had the political means, for
their large concentration in urban centers gave them strategic
capabilities to influence the outcome of close elections.

Even though Negro aspirations for greater human equality were rising, the military establishment seemed to turn a
deaf ear to their complaints. There were three important

reasons for this.   One was the ingrained belief of Negro combat inferiority.   The men in responsible leadership positions
in the Pentagon had been brought up on the belief that integration would seriously impair military effectiveness.   A
string of military reports since World War I had hardened
these attitudes into rigid military policy.

Second, every service school had taught the Army leadership not to meddle in politics, and the soldiering profession
regarded integration as clearly political. [37]   The fear of intro-
ducing a social reform and of alienating Southern conservatives arose at the mere suggestion of integration.   And in the
years before the Brown Decision, integration was a pretty
startling suggestion even to the average white American.

Finally, military leaders rather than civilians domi-
nated the Pentagon. [38]   The Eisenhowers, Bradleys, and
Nimitzes ran the Defense Department rather than their civilian Secretaries, because the military leaders were the popular war heroes.   Thus, the civilians who could be more responsive to the political climate were prisoners of military
racial opinion.

Shortly after World War II, Eisenhower, as Army Chief
of Staff, established a board of officers to recommend how the
military should use Negroes in peacetime.   The board was
headed by Alvan C. Gillem, 13th Army Corps Commander,
and included three other Army generals.   The Gillem Report
was published March 4, 1946, and entitled "Utilization of Negro Manpower in the Postwar Army Policy. "[39]   The findings
were a logical consequence of the three factors outlined in the
preceding paragraphs.   The report's major points were: 1)
maintenance of a 10-per-cent quota for Negroes; 2) employment of Negroes in regimental-size units or smaller, rather
than divisions; 3) the promise of encouraging expansion of the
number of Negro officers; 4) utilization of skilled NCO's in
overhead and special units permitting limited integration; 5)
assignment of Negro units to locales where sentiments were
favorable to colored personnel; 6) integration of on-base buses,
recreational facilities, and officers' messes, where this policy would not infringe on local custom.

Eisenhower approved the recommendations but the effects of the report were not what the military had envisioned.
The 10-per-cent quota shut off recruitment of Negroes for six

months during 1946 because the military colored quota was full. This provoked a sharp attack by Roy Wilkins of the NAACP and a rash of court cases challenging the military limitation. [40] There was no appreciable change in on-post integration or Negro officer recruitment, nor did senior skilled colored NCO's find jobs in white units. And while the Negro 24th Regiment was stationed in Japan with the 25th Division, many smaller training units remained in the South, in the locale of high segregation, producing racial tensions.

The Gillem Board Report was intended to resolve the use of Negroes in the Army--as visualized by the Army generals. Its failure was due not to the Board but to the soldiering profession. The lack of critical thought on racial matters and the uncompromising view that all Negroes were inferior soldiers had led to the 10-per-cent quota and maintenance of segregated units. The military in steering clear of politics failed to comprehend the Negro attitude and indulged in the false hope that their status quo philosophy would be tolerated.

In the postwar Navy, Secretary James Forrestal was seriously convinced that integration was the right course. In two administrative orders, he attempted to achieve this objective. In December, 1945, he issued an order to all ships and stations: "In the administration of Naval personnel, no differentiation shall be made because of race or color. This applies also to authorized personnel of all the Armed Forces aboard Navy ships."[41] On February 27, 1946, Forrestal sent out a circular letter to all commanders, ordering: "Effective immediately, all restrictions governing types of assignments for which Negro Naval personnel are eligible are hereby lifted. Henceforth, they shall be eligible for all types of assignments in all ratings in all activities and all ships of the Naval service.... In utilization of housing, messing and other facilities, no special or unusual provisions will be made for the accommodation of Negroes.[42]

Despite these two bold statements evidencing Forrestal's deep commitment to racial equality in the Navy, the Negro community was not to be easily persuaded that the Navy's attitudes had really changed. Few sought officers' or skilled NCO jobs. In April, 1946, out of the Navy's 19,102 Negroes, 83 per cent were in the stewards' branch and only twenty-four were

chief petty officers and three were officers. Making reforms
was not enough: The Navy had to convince Negroes that reforms had actually been made. [43]

Nevertheless, this was the first attempt at permanent
integration of the armed forces, and it was the achievement
of the civilian Secretary James Forrestal, not the admirals.
Why was Secretary Forrestal the man to introduce integration
in the armed forces? The reason lies in the nature of the man,
which is described by Robert Albion and Robert Connery:

> The mixture of the intellectual and the astute
> businessman in Forrestal presented a pattern
> that was unusual in executives. He was a
> much more effective executive than many of
> those who held that post, and his experience
> gives a pretty good picture of how an efficient
> Secretary operates, the kind of people he sees,
> the questions that come to him for decision,
> the quality of the staff he has, and in general,
> the environment in which he works. [44]

Forrestal was an independent intellect who could be
skeptical of the arguments that the Negro could learn only the
skills of messman and that integration would reduce ship
efficiency. He was an executive who realized how racial
tensions harm organizational efficiency and how human talents
could be better employed in the Navy if ability, rather than race,
determined who went where and who did what. More important,
he had the knack to get what he wanted because he had established strong civilian control of his admirals.

Two significant developments occurred at the end of
1947. On October 30, President Truman's Civil Rights Committee issued its report, To Secure These Rights. Almost
unnoticed, one short paragraph of it urged elimination of segregation in the armed forces. [45] Service leadership paid it no
attention. Nor did the military heed the rising political tem-
peratures in the Negro community. On November 23, 1947,
A. Phillip Randolph, president of the Brotherhood of Sleeping
Car Porters, and Grant Reynolds, a former Harlem Republican City Councilman, organized the Committee Against Jim
Crow in Military Service and Training, with their headquarters
at the New York Sleeping Car Porters union office. [46] Both
men, noted Negro political activists, were seizing upon an

issue that all Negroes knew about and could be easily aroused
by--segregation in the armed forces. While undoubtedly this
was a politically expedient move, Randolph and Reynolds
gained the support of nearly all Negroes--North and South,
upper class and lower class. They had the backing of almost
every Negro newspaper, as well as many prominent colored
leaders, like Carter G. Woodson, Alair Locke, W.H. Jernagin,
Channing Tobias, George S. Schuyler, Joe Louis, and Emma
Clarissa. [47]

The issue of armed forces segregation hung in abeyance
until 1948. Then, due to increased Army personnel requirements to cope with widening world commitments, the Joint
Chiefs of Staff asked Congress for a draft law early in March.
That month, Randolph told President Truman: "Negroes do
not want to shoulder a gun to fight for democracy abroad un-
less full democracy was obtained at home."[48] Randolph described the President's reaction a week later at an NAACP
rally: "It was most unwelcome news to him."[49]

The showdown came March 31, when Randolph and Reynolds testified before the Senate Armed Services Committee
hearings on the draft bill. Randolph bluntly announced: "Today I would like to make clear to this committee and through
you to Congress and the American people that passage now of
a Jim Crow draft may only result in mass civil disobedience."[50]
These were the days before marches, sit-ins, and stall-ins,
and such words from a Negro inflamed the committee Senators.
"It may well lead to indictments of treason,"[51] snapped Republican Wayne Morse.

Randolph's threat had raised the issue to national prom-
inence--forcing the military and politicians to take note of
Negro demands. But the threat was largely bluff, for the
anti-Jim Crow committee's influence was limited in leadership, short on financial resources, and lacked organized
massive Negro community support.

Randolph's approach was disavowed by Roy Wilkins of
the NAACP, and thirteen presidents of Negro colleges announced their opposition.[52] The New York Negro Communist
Benjamin J. Davis called Randolph a "troublemaker" and
"headline grabber," and accused him of spreading "confusion,
division, and defeatism among the Negro people."[53] Before
the same Senate Committee, Truman K. Gibson, Jr., a

former War Department aide, referred to Randolph's and Reynolds' plan to eliminate Jim Crow in the military as "cynical bargaining" with patriotism. [54] But the caustic comments of the anti-Jim Crow committee silenced most Negroes who disagreed with it. Grant Reynolds quickly called Gibson "a War Department mouthpiece. "[55] Congressional Southerners were of further help in the anti-Jim Crow committee's efforts to quiet Uncle Toms. Senator Richard B. Russell of Georgia expounded on how much he preferred patriotic Negroes to men like Randolph--just the sort of condemnation to boost Randolph's stock among colored citizens. [56]

The military found themselves in an uncomfortable corner. On April 2, the Senate Committee asked General Dwight D. Eisenhower about the Army's position on segregation. He replied: "There is race prejudice in this country ... When you pass a law to get somebody to like someone, you have trouble. "[57] The emptiness of his rhetoric was so apparent that it only aroused more sympathy for the colored cause.

Soon groups like the Urban League, the NAACP, the ADA, and the Jewish War Veterans declared themselves against military segregation. In Congress, Adam C. Powell and Jacob K. Javits proposed anti-segregation amendments to the draft bill. [58] They were both defeated, 102-14 and 135-23. Powell attacked Gibson: "Negro veterans and their families will always remember Gibson as the rubber-stamp Uncle Tom who was used by the War Department to cast aspersions on Negro troops in Italy while those same Negroes were shedding their blood and dying. "[59]

Senator Russell proposed an amendment to the draft bill that would permit men to choose units of their own race. [60] The measure was defeated by the Armed Services Committee.

Although on June 24, 1948, President Truman signed the draft law without either Southern or Negro amendments, the process of getting the legislation through Congress had enabled Negro voices to be heard. Now in the Negro camp the forces were going through the motions of carrying out their threatened "mass civil disobedience. " Grant Reynolds, from the New York headquarters of the Brotherhood of Sleeping Car Porters, announced: "Negroes would be prepared to face prison rather than join a Jim Crow Army. "[61] A Newsweek poll showed 71 per cent of Negro college youth favored the

Randolph philosophy of "mass civil disobedience. "[62] The
anti-Jim Crow committee announced that it would 1) cam-
paign to persuade Negro youths to openly refuse to register;
2) obtain lawyers to defend those caught for draft evasion; and
3) distribute buttons and pamphlets with the theme, "Don't
Join a Jim Crow Army. "[63]

A further source of Negro discontent was an April 26
meeting between Secretary of the Army Kenneth C. Royall and
sixteen Negro leaders--Lester B. Granger, Mrs. Sadie T. M.
Alexander, Dr. John W. Davis, Truman K. Gibson, Jr.,
Charles H. Houston, Bishop J. W. Gregg, the Reverend John
H. Johnson, Dr. Mordecai Johnson, P. B. Young, Ira F.
Lewis, Dr. B. E. Mays, Loren Miller, Hobson E. Reynolds,
Dr. Channing H. Tobias, George L. P. Weaver, and Roy
Wilkins. The Negroes had come to hear the Army's views
and to encourage changes in military policy. But Royall,
deeply influenced by the attitudes of the generals surrounding
him, was unyielding: "Any improvement must be made within
the framework of segregation. " The colored leaders went
away feeling that they had encountered "a brick wall. "[64]

Politicians uneasily watched the rising Negro dissatisfaction. The Republicans at their convention in late June
attempted to pacify the Negroes' interests by offering a weak
civil-rights program that included a promise to end segregation in the armed forces. [65] Eyes turned toward the Demo-
crats when they met in mid-July. Seeking to maintain party
unity, Truman at first sided with the Southern conservatives
against a strong civil-rights plank in the Democratic platform.
However, in a Convention revolt led by Mayor Hubert H.
Humphrey of Minneapolis, the liberals pushed through a strong
civil-rights plank over Truman's objections. The Southerners,
headed by Senator Russell, walked out of the convention, and
Truman, left with a liberal platform and liberal political support, switched to what became a winning strategy of aggres-
sively seeking minority votes. [66]

Upon returning to the White House from the convention,
the President summoned his two racial advisers, Philleo Nash
and Clifford Ewing. The product of their efforts was Executive
Order 9981, requiring equal opportunity in the armed forces
regardless of race, signed July 26, 1948. (The full text appears on
the following pages.)[67]

Executive Order 9981

Whereas it is essential that there be maintained in the Armed Services of the United States the highest standards of democracy, with equality of treatment and opportunity for all those who serve in our country's defense:

Now, therefore, by virtue of the authority vested in me as President of the United States, and as Commander in Chief of the Armed Services, it is ordered as follows:

1. It is hereby declared to be the policy of the President that there shall be equality of treatment and opportunity for all persons in the Armed Services without regard to race, color, religion or national origin. This policy shall be put into effect as rapidly as possible, having due regard to the time required to effectuate any necessary changes without impairing the efficiency or morale.

2. There shall be created in the National Military Establishment an advisory committee to be known as the President's Committee on Equality of Treatment and Opportunity in the Armed Services which shall be composed of seven members to be designated by the President.

3. The committee is authorized on behalf of the President to examine into the rules, procedures, and practices of the Armed Services in order to determine in what respect such rules, procedures and practices may be altered or improved with a view to carrying out the policy of this order. The committee shall confer and advise with the Secretary of Defense, the Secretary of the Navy, and the Secretary of the Air Force and shall make such recommendations to the President and to said Secretaries as in the judgment of the committee will effectuate the policy hereof.

4. All Executive departments and agencies of the Federal Government are authorized and directed to cooperate with the committee in its work, and to furnish the committee with such information or the services of such persons as the committee may require in the performance of its duties.

5.   When requested by the committee to do so, persons in the Armed Services or in any of the Executive departments and agencies of the Federal Government shall testify before the committee and shall make available for the use of the committee such documents and other information as the committee may require.

6.   The committee shall continue to exist until such time as the President shall terminate its existence by Executive Order.

HARRY S. TRUMAN

Signed July 26, 1948

Source: The New York Times, July 27, 1948, p. 4.

For Negroes, the order was an enormous political victory. Randolph said: "It substantially fulfilled my demands on the President. "[68] The jubilant Reynolds in a Nation article hailed it as a "triumph for civil disobedience. "[69] By the end of August, the Committee Against Jim Crow in Military Service and Training had folded.

The military leadership was not happy. The New York Times military analyst, Hanson Baldwin, wrote that Army Chief of Staff, Omar Bradley, feared that using the armed forces as a "tool for social justice" would jeopardize military effectiveness. [70]

In reality, Executive Order 9981 was not as drastic a reform as either the military or the Negroes believed. It was primarily an excellent political move by Truman to gain Negro votes on Election Day. It promised not integration but "equality of treatment and opportunity, " an ill-defined generality. Moreover, it did not specify when "equality of treatment and opportunity" would occur. The most important achievement of 9981 was establishment of the Committee on Equality of Treatment and Opportunity in the Armed Forces, which was an important means of stimulating discussion of military racial policies, a subject long avoided by officers. But even the future of the committee was not assured until Truman's surprising re-election in November.

When the President signed the Executive Order, colored leadership ended the prospect of draft evasion. The Negroes had won a major political victory on a shrewdly selected issue. Military civil rights was an issue that could unify many diverse types of Negroes. No matter what their geographic, economic, or social backgrounds, most Negroes knew of or had personally experienced military segregation, and so they shared a common goal. And the goal was relatively easy to achieve, for it demanded nothing from the majority of white Americans, unlike asking an end to discrimination in employment, where blacks and whites are pitted in direct competition for economic benefits. Furthermore, the military was an easy target, for it was the only major source of governmental discrimination. Although the State Department, Civil Service, and other federal agencies had racial problems, only the armed services displayed segregation on a large scale. It was easy to criticize this department, while it was not so clear what to do about the others.

Thus, in 1948 the Negroes flexed their political muscles by a wise choice of issue that was clear cut and capable of mobilizing Negroes across-the-board without alienating the white majority.

ADMINISTRATIVE POLITICS, 1949-50

By 1949, the important battles were being fought inside the Defense Department. Early in the year, the President's Committee on Equality of Treatment and Opportunity in the Armed Forces, appointed in September, began to function actively. It was chaired by a former U.S. Solicitor General, Charles H. Fahy, and its six other members were two whites who did not participate, two whites who were sympathetic to Negro problems, and two Negroes who had had experience in armed-forces racial problems. They included, A.J. Donahue of Stamford, Connecticut, president of the A.J. Donahue Corporation; Dwight R.G. Palmer of New York, president of General Cable Corporation; Charles Luckman of Cambridge, Massachusetts, president of Lever Brothers; William E. Stevenson of Oberlin, Ohio, president of Oberlin College; Lester Granger of New York, executive secretary of the National Urban League; and John H. Sengstacke of Chicago, publisher of the Chicago Defender.[71]

The importance of the Fahy Committee cannot be over-rated. It succeeded in bringing civilian views into the nation's defense organization, long handicapped by the dominance of the military and its rigidity of thought on racial affairs. The presence of the committee, until May, 1950, institutionalized Presidential interest in improving the status of Negro personnel within the Pentagon. Its presence engendered a dialogue on a subject long considered incapable of discussion by officers, and publicized alternatives to the segregation policy. Also, it served as a base for collecting quantitative data on Negro service participation and a place for forming alliances with friendly Defense administrators and finding and checking resistance to the Presidential Order.

An alliance with one Defense administrator was indispensable to the effectiveness of the Fahy Committee. Early in 1949, Louis B. Johnson was appointed Secretary of Defense, succeeding the ailing James Forrestal. Johnson was an ambitious political activist and a partisan Democrat.[72] Convinced by the committee of the importance of the race issue, he interpreted Executive Order 9981 to call for integration in the services here and now. Thus Johnson, on April 24, 1949, announced: 1) detailed proposals for ending racial separation were required from each service; 2) the deadlines for each service to submit its integration plans; and 3) James C. Evans's appointment as his personal aide on racial problems. [73]

The Air Force made the speediest response. Established as a separate department from the Army under the 1947 unification plan, it was staffed by younger, more adaptable officers. Few of them had been involved in the long development of the Army's racial policy since World War I and many of them remembered the recent heroism of the all-colored 332nd Fighter Group. The new Air Secretary was Stuart Symington, another ambitious, politically active Democrat. His business training and strong personality asserted effective civilian control over the new department, and he tried hard to follow the spirit of the Truman order. [74]

Initially, the Air Force had followed the Army's policy of a 10-per-cent quota and separate facilities for blacks. However, the new organization was eager to develop its own identity, and when Symington polled the field commanders early in the year, he found them to be generally receptive to integration, particularly since it could alleviate the shortage of skilled personnel--the colored units had an abundance of the skilled individuals that the white units found in short supply. [75]

After one meeting with the Fahy Committee, the Air Force submitted its plan for integration to Johnson, which he approved on May 11. It consisted of five points: 1) the break-up of the major all-colored unit, the 332nd Fighter Group at Lockbourne Field, would start within ten days; skilled personnel would be shifted to other assignments and nonskilled men would be discharged; 2) the few small Negro support units would be broken up as soon as possible; 3) the 10-per-cent quota on enlistments would end; 4) field commanders would be notified of the department's new policy and the strong desire to have it carried out smoothly; 5) the Air Force would closely follow the progress of integration by corresponding with individual commanders and by making General Idwal S. Edwards and Colonel Benjamin O. Davis, Jr., responsible for the project. [76]

Air Force administrators worked efficiently, and in eight months 75 per cent of its 25,000 Negroes were integrated. In January, 1950, the European Air Force Commander reported "complete acceptance of the Negro as a co-equal."[77] Abolishing the 10-per-cent quota, contrary to many fears, resulted in only a slight rise (.13 per cent) in the percentage of Negroes in the Air Force.[78]

Although of all three services the Air Force had the highest proportion of lower-middle-class individuals (the group that sociologists have shown to have the highest prejudice against Negroes),[79] the Air Force demonstrated that strong civilian leadership and dedicated military officers could bring about swift integration. The Air Force had several advantages over the Army and Navy. It had a lower percentage of Negroes: 6 per cent compared to the Army's 10 per cent.[80] A higher proportion of its Negroes were skilled, and thus more easily transferred to other jobs in the organizational structure.[81] And skilled individuals were then in high demand in the Air Force. Also, unlike the other services, the Air Force had the bulk of its Negroes in one place, at Lockbourne, and it was administratively easier to break up one unit and obtain a higher percentage of integrated troops. Thus, the Air Force record looked good almost immediately, since it had fewer segregated units to disband. Finally, the new department genuinely desired to make a better record than the Army and Navy. Army Secretary Royall complained: "They are trying to show up the Army."[82]

Although the Navy, under Forrestal's leadership had been the first service to reform its racial policy and had ended all forms of separation early in 1946, it still had too many Negro stewards and too few Negro officers. After several meetings between Navy representatives and the Fahy Committee, Secretary Johnson on June 7 approved a six-point plan for the Navy. Its provisions were to 1) issue a policy statement on minorities; 2) attract more Negroes to the Navy through better publicity; 3) encourage more Negroes to apply for NROTC; 4) permit men to transfer easily from the stewards' branch; 5) change the status of chief of stewards to chief petty officers; and 6) eliminate separate Marine and Navy basic training.[83]

Unlike the Air Force, the Navy could not find swift administrative solutions. It needed skilled men, but its colored

sailors were unskilled messmen. The Navy wanted Negroes
in higher officer ranks, but it takes twenty years to attain the
captain's grade and the first Negro officers had been commissioned only five years before. The Navy leadership had
a serious desire to provide better opportunity for Negroes,
but its historic image, projected to the Negro since Navy
Secretary Stoddert's order in 1798, of being a closed, caste-
conscious body was not easily erased. It was partly the Negro's fault for continuing to believe in the lingering myth of
Navy exclusion and rejecting the advances made by Forrestal.
Equally, it was the Navy's fault for not making a greater effort to publicize its accomplishments to the minority. And
what was concurrently happening in the Air Force was only
making it tougher for the Navy to attract and hold on to the
kind of Negroes it wanted.

The May, 1950, Fahy Committee Report emphasized the
advances the Navy had made. Over five years, the Navy had
moved from complete exclusion of Negroes from the general
service to where 52 per cent of its Negroes were outside the
stewards' branch. From 1949 to 1950, the Navy increased
its number of colored officers from 4 to 17. [84] But the report
expressed dissatisfaction that so few sought entrance into the
Holloway Program or into Annapolis. (The Holloway Program
established four-year college scholarships for young men who
agreed to take naval training in college and, upon graduation,
serve in the regular Navy for at least four years.) E.W. Kenworthy, secretary of the Fahy Committee, wrote in a New
York Times Magazine article, that the Navy's "obligation to
make fair words good continues. "[85] But Kenworthy begged
the question. If the Navy's words were good and its actions
were good, how did you make Negroes believe them and en-
list? A communication gap existed between Navy and Negro.
Each mistrusted the other, and this schism of over a century
could not be healed by instant administrative actions.

The Army's situation, from 1947 until early 1949, was
the result of Secretary Kenneth C. Royall's submission to the
conservative fears of his generals. Omar Bradley felt that
integration of the Army's large percentage of Negroes would
cause a serious decline in fighting effectiveness. George
Marshall foresaw that if the Army ended segregation, the
number of Negroes would rise until they made up one-third of
the ranks, driving whites out of uniform. [86]

Why did Royall surrender to his officers' racial opinions more readily than Forrestal or Symington? Perhaps personality was an important factor. Also, Royall was overshadowed by the glory of the military advisers surrounding him. [87] But as Professor Samuel P. Huntington hypothesizes, [88] the vertical structure of the Army organization made the civilian Secretary highly dependent on the advice of his Chief of Staff, who was in the direct chain of command. Both the logistical-support branches and the field commanders were responsible to the military Chief of Staff, and the civilian Secretary went through him to influence Army functions. The Navy's structure was different. Each bureau chief reported directly to the civilian Secretary as well as the Chief of Naval Operations, who commanded the fleet. The Navy's balanced organization permitted the Secretary to hear more officer viewpoints than the Army's vertical pattern, which encouraged the Chief of Staff to speak for the military body.

The nature of military organization which made the civilian Secretary dependent on his Chief of Staff's racial views was a principal reason why Secretary of Defense Johnson turned down the Army's proposed plans for integration on May 11, June 20, and July 11, calling them either "too vague" or "still failing to meet the basic intent of Executive Order 9981."[89] During this period, Gordon Gray was appointed Army Secretary. Gray succeeded in prodding the Army to announce, on October 1, a program that gained approval by the Fahy Committee and Secretary Louis Johnson. It promised to 1) abolish quotas for units and schools; 2) develop a new promotion system based on competition without regard to race; 3) conduct ROTC summer-camp training without regard to race; 4) establish a board of Army officers to review Negro policies; and 5) retain segregated units but give qualified Negroes the opportunity to gain skills previously unattainable and assign Negroes who had acquired skills to positions where their specialties might be applied in a manner useful to the military. [90]

It is surprising that the Fahy Committee and Johnson accepted these limited proposals. But Gray could not carry out even these circumscribed plans. Late in the month, he discovered a military order rescinding these proposals, and in November he reissued the same October 1 proposal. [91] On January 16, 1950, he issued still another order declaring that skilled personnel would be assigned to units regardless of

race or color, adding that commanders would be held responsible for any attempt to evade this order. [92] Gray, like Royall before him, found that the generals' racial views pre-
vailed over the department rather than being subordinate to
the Secretary's policy. When the Fahy Committee completed
its work in May, 1950, the 60,000 colored Army personnel
were still in segregated units, with only paper promises of
integration. It was to take the Korean War to change this
situation.

THE KOREAN WAR, 1950-53

Korea stimulated a breath-taking leap in the Army's attitude toward Negroes. It was a change taken not because the
generals felt any new benevolence toward the Negro but because of very real professional needs: 1) training efficiency,
2) combat-line strength, 3) unit uniformity, 4) equality of
opportunity for battlefield casualty.

Army training can teach many men many skills very
rapidly. And, when local Army commanders found that training efficiency was being handicapped by segregation, they discovered that it was to their own advantage to integrate because it speeded the learning of their recruits. Journalist
Lee Nichols described what happened at Fort Jackson:

> Fort Jackson, South Carolina, under orders to
> close in the spring of 1950, was reactivated as
> a major infantry training base. Brigadier Gen-
> eral Frank McConnell was chosen to set up and
> command the 8th U.S. Infantry Division to train
> draftees.
>
> He had been expected to set up a separate
> organization to train Negro inductees, and had
> received a special training cadre or staff of
> Negro and white officers and non-coms from
> Fort Dix, New Jersey, to handle the job.
>
> The first draftees arrived in August. "I
> tried to sort them by color," McConnell said,
> "but they began pouring in more rapidly; we got
> up to 1,000 recruits a day. Arriving without

any pattern, busloads of Negroes, then busloads
of whites, it was totally impractical to sort
them out."

McConnell conferred with his staff and proposed to put the Negroes and whites into platoons
together. A staff member expressed fear
McConnell might be "going off the deep end,"
suggested a check with General Mark W. Clark,
Chief of U.S. Army Field Forces.

"I pulled out the Army announcement on
non-segregation," recounted McConnell. This
was Gray's order of January 1950. "It was
all the authority I needed. I said that if we
didn't ask permission, they couldn't stop us."
However, he telephoned Lt. General John R.
Hodge, an old friend and commander of the 3rd
Army which included Fort Jackson, and informed
him "about the same day, he was all for it, and
considered it a practical thing to do."

McConnell issued instructions that the next
fifty-five draftees who arrived, regardless of
color, would be formed into a platoon, and the
same with subsequent arrivals. The order was
issued verbally, he said, "and that was the end
of segregation at Fort Jackson."[93]

McConnell was not the first Army commander to take
the initiative and integrate because he felt it was the best way
to run an Army. Andrew Jackson drafted blacks in 1814 to
protect New Orleans, and the commander at Port Royal, South
Carolina, in 1862 defied Lincoln's orders and included Negroes.
Eisenhower, in 1945, integrated his forces because of manpower
needs. And on many posts during the Korean War, commanders could not affort the luxury of segregation when they were
required to rapidly train many men, one-tenth of whom were
colored.

Second, the first year of combat in Korea convinced the
Army that all-Negro units were a serious handicap to line
strength. They were the weak link, requiring extra rein-
forcements and provoking the enemy to attack them as the
point where the line would crumble most easily. Negro units,

the Army found, whether in division or squad size, performed less effectively than all-white or integrated units.
Uniform line strength is essential in fighting, since weak
points are the first avenues to defeat. This inferiority in combat ability of all-Negro units, and its vulnerability to the
enemy, worried military leadership the most.

Brigadier General J. H. Michealis, who observed the
all-Negro 24th Regiment in combat from July 10, 1950, to
May 5, 1951, concluded:

> It is the writer's conviction that a Negro unit,
> whether it be a squad, platoon, company or
> battalion, is incapable of producing satisfactory
> results during periods of sustained combat.
> Despite the selection of the best available
> officers and in the early phases, non-com-
> missioned white officers, Negro units of the 24th
> Infantry Regiment repeatedly demonstrated
> their inability to either secure an objective
> against determined resistance or to defend,
> particularly at night against enemy attack of
> any size. Repeated examples exist of successful
> North Korean attacks against Negro companies
> and battalions for the sole purpose of securing
> American weapons and ammunition--the North
> Korean attack being unsupported by the heavier
> weapons, and the Koreans themselves armed
> only with grenades. Under ideal conditions
> during daylight with excessive assistance from
> supporting Army, the Negro unit can secure a
> limited objective.

> To summarize, the Negro units, regardless
> of size, in combat are not successful, and are a
> liability to adjacent units.

> During the bitter holding action of last August
> on the Pusan perimeter, the repeated failures of
> the 24th Infantry became so critical, the Division
> Commander, Major General W. B. Kean, in order
> to bolster this Regiment, placed approximately
> 250 Negro enlisted men with each white Regiment
> and in turn from the pipeline placed volunteer
> white non-commissioned officers with the 24th

Infantry. This 250 amounted to approximately
ten per cent of the then existing strength of the
white Regiments. These Negroes were integrated down to the lowest tactical unit, the
squad, and in this capacity have proved satisfactory. Some have been promoted, others have
been decorated. I mention this to point out the
fact that there is no color line in a foxhole.
Apparently, the white soldier has no objection
to serving under a Negro NCO, if the NCO has
proved himself in battle. Specifically, although
nine white battalions cannot hold one Negro
battalion on a hill, it appears to me that this
incapability of a Negro unit to fight is founded
in the Negro's lack of respect for his fellow
Negro. He does not trust the Negro in the
adjacent foxhole, whereas he does have confidence in the white soldier in the adjacent
foxhole.

In my opinion, intellectual attainment and
stamina on the battlefield are directly related.
I believe that some five per cent of the Negro
population of the 24th Infantry Regiment made
outstanding and valorous leaders and that another
20 per cent were excellent followers. The percentages in white regiments are considerably
higher. I believe these percentages are closely
related to the higher intellectual level attained
by any given group of whites. In other words,
the reasonably intelligent Negro will make an
effective Infantryman. [94]

Professional Army opinion was not alone in its estima-
tion of Negro combat abilities. An article, much criticized in
the Negro press as "slander," written by a journalist, Harold
H. Martin, who spent some time in Korea observing the 24th,
appeared in the Saturday Evening Post of June 16, 1951:

The enemy was well aware of the Regiment's
tendency to break when attacked at night, and in
the fighting around Pusan, according to Negro
Korean prisoners, they would make supply
attacks on the 24th when they needed weapons. [95]

Martin pointed out that the 24th drew in one week 956 rifles, while its sister regiments, the 27th and 35th, drew 100 and 270 rifles, respectively.

Even the three-volume report of Project CLEAR, a Study of the Utilization of Negro Manpower, prepared by the Operations Research Office of Johns Hopkins University and published on June 30, 1951, concluded, not that Negro units were effective in combat, but that personnel in these outfits could be utilized better on an integrated basis:

> Integration of Negro and white personnel in Korea has been successful to the extent that it has been put into effect. Where Negroes have been mixed into white units it has proceeded smoothly without conflict. There is over-whelming opinion among officers that Negroes should serve in both mixed and combat units on an integrated basis. [96]

But the Army profession's view that Negro units were poorer than white ones implied that the individual Negro soldier was inferior, which caused considerable dissatisfaction among Negroes in America. However, both Generals Matthew B. Ridgeway and James A. Van Fleet had praised the exploits of the two Negro Medal of Honor winners in Korea, William Thompson and Cornelius Charlton. [97] Lieutenant Colonel J. T. Corley said, upon assuming command of the 24th Infantry after the unit had been fighting in Korea since July 12, 1950:

> Upon assumption of command, I cannot help but express my opinion of the fighting 24th Infantry. In sixty days of continuous combat, you have withstood a roughness of battle which I had not seen in five campaigns in Africa, Sicily and Europe with the First Infantry Division. You have held ground against superior odds. You have lived up to the regimental motto "Semper Paratus." The first United States victory in Korea was your action at Yech'on. It has been noted in Congress. [98]

The organization of the units, not the men, had been inferior. Segregated groupment stimulated tensions between whites and blacks, causing a weaker unit than integrated groupment, which placed men by ability, not by race.

Professional soldiers recognized segregated groupment in combat as a serious tactical weakness and saw that integration was the logical solution. And so it happened that on July 31, 1950, Commander of United Nations Forces in Korea Matthew B. Ridgeway obtained from the Pentagon the authority to integrate Negro units in his combat zone. [99]

Third, the Army's passion for unit uniformity influenced the integration of the rest of its forces. It was hard for the Army to reconcile the fact that half of its forces were integrated at troop-training centers and in the Korean combat zone while its forces in Europe and the rest of continental America remained segregated. Thus, in April, 1952, the European Command issued orders to break up twenty-five Negro units within a month. Ernest Leiser, a journalist, described the integration of the 272nd all-colored 600-man Artillery Battalion early in April. [100] In January, 1950, the 272nd had been noted for its "low morale" and "slack discipline." When the orders to integrate were received, the unit sent 20 per cent of those about ready to return home to Bremerhaven, the port of embarkation. Twenty per cent of the key officers and senior enlisted personnel remained in the unit to form the nucleus of a newly integrated staff. Sixty per cent went on a Seventh Army roster, where they were divided in four packets of men and sent out to other troop units; in turn, the 272nd received four groups of white troops from other artillery units.

The integration move was forcefully backed by the commanding officers of the units. Colonel Ralph Swicker, 18th Infantry regimental commander, told his unit which was about to be integrated: "Now men, I want you to understand this clearly because it's an order. In this integration program there will be no trouble. "[101] Lieutenant Colonel Jack S. Blocker, the white commander of the 272nd, emphasized: "This is what your people have wanted for a long time. Now whether it works or is a monumental foulup is going to depend very considerably on you. "[102]

After the change, Leiser observed that the 272nd had become a stronger combat organization:

> Integration has already eliminated those weak
> spots in the line. The new 272nd smarted up and
> straightened out almost immediately. Its in-
> cident rate dropped and its efficiency rating rose.
>
> I did not find any white commanders who
> reported that the efficiency or morale of their
> unit as a whole had dropped to any great extent
> since the influx of Negroes. [103]

Why were the conservative Southerners in Congress silent on what was happening in the defense establishment? Why
did not powerful conservatives in armed-services committees
in Senate and House oppose the reforms?

The reason is found in the response of military congressional liaisons to legislative queries about integration. They
emphasized it was not equal treatment of the Negro, but equal
opportunity for battlefield casualty. It was a simple argument
that if Negroes were not given equal chances for combat, more
whites would be on the casualty lists. To a Congressman sensitive about the lives of his constituents' sons, the words were
persuasive. [104]

This reasoning is found in a statement by Brigadier General John H. Michaelis:

> Because national welfare demands proportionate
> losses of its varied manpower, I am convinced
> that controlled integration of Negro personnel
> into white combat units in proportion to the Negro
> population of the Army is mandatory. This per-
> centage, around 11 or 12 per cent, does not
> materially reduce combat effectiveness of the
> white combat unit and if maintained at this level
> and no higher will insure effective utilization of
> Negro manpower. [105]

But why was this concept--that all-Negro units were ineffective and should be integrated to improve line strength--accepted
in Korea but not in World War I and World War II? The problem was that until then the alternatives had never been presented as clearly to the military profession. Thus, the goals
of the Negro community and the Truman order were achieved
in the Army between 1950 and 1953, not because of any ideals
of colored equality but because of the pragmatic demands of the
professional soldier.

CHAPTER THE POST-KOREAN
ERA

THE RESULTS OF INTEGRATION

By the end of the Korean War, the Army was virtually
integrated. By January 1, 1954, of the 250,000 Negroes in
the Army, only 10,000 were in small scattered segregated
units. Within a year, even these had disappeared. James
Evans, Pentagon civil-rights counselor, formally announced
on October 31, 1954, that no all-colored units remained. [1]
In addition, during the Korean War, all the Air Force's 66,000
Negroes had been integrated. In the summer of 1952, the
Marines had disbanded their last Negro units; however, two-
fifths of the Navy's Negroes still remained in the stewards'
branch. [2] To ensure greater equality, Defense administrators
in 1954 took minor actions--eliminating segregation in post-
operated schools, deleting the Negro classification on personnel forms, and abolishing separate recruitment of Negroes
for the stewards' branch. [3]

Effects of this integration, apparent inside and outside
the military, included: 1) an increased commitment to military integration by national political candidates; 2) a reduction
of Negro community hostility toward the military; 3) long-run
structural improvement in the Defense establishment; 4) general support for integration by military leaders; and 5) more
influence on military than civilian life.

National Political Candidates' Commitment to Military Integration

The two major-party candidates in 1952 and 1956 attempted to outdo each other in committing themselves to
military integration. Campaigning for Stevenson, President
Truman on October 29, 1952, pointed to his executive order
of 1948 as proof of the Democratic Party's dedication to integration. Truman recalled Stevenson's record in working to

end segregation both in the Navy Department during World
War II and, as Governor of Illinois, in his state's National
Guard. [4] General Eisenhower replied the next day in a New
York address, saying: "As President, I will see to it that we
end all discrimination... in the armed forces. "[5]

In the 1956 election, there was another round of both
major-party candidates pledging themselves to military integration. In a speech on October 4, 1956, before a Harlem
audience, Stevenson repeated Truman's accomplishments and
his own role in ending military segregation. [6] Stevenson was
replying to a speech given two days earlier by President
Eisenhower, in which he had declared: "Genuine progress has
been made in eliminating racial segregation... in the armed
forces. "[7]

The argument over who had done more reflected the
necessity for both Democratic and Republican leadership to
appease the important pressures of the Negro community as
well as gain the backing of a generally approving white America. While just ten years earlier it would have been unsound
strategy to argue for integration, in 1952 and 1956 it was im-
perative. The weakness of the political discussion was that
while all committed themselves to the existing program, few
were willing to explore the new problems arising out of the
Negro-military relationship.

Reduction of the Negro Community's
Hostility Toward the Military

After military integration, criticism by Negro protest
organizations, publications, and Congressmen declined.
Ebony magazine, a worthy gauge of middle-class Negro opinion, published several stories depicting the equal status of
colored soldiers in the armed forces. In "Every GI a King, "
Ebony described Pfc. Timothy Fox of Summerfield, North
Carolina, who was stationed in Japan, as "a man who never
had it so good. "[8] The NAACP, the oldest colored protest organization, at its June 28, 1953, and December 30, 1954,
national conventions, officially praised the armed services
for their policies of integration. [9]

Within the service, Negroes seemed to have fewer complaints. As Army Sergeant First Class John Lawrence told
a Reporter magazine correspondent at Fort Jackson, South

Carolina: "A lot of us Negroes never had it so good. A corporal can make $1,000 by re-enlisting, buy a car and live big. The young Negro in uniform feels big in it. It shows he's an American and that he's as good as anyone else."[10] As Private C. C. Moskos of the 9th Engineer Battalion, U.S. Army, wrote for Negro History Bulletin: "The thickness of a man's lips is not a factor when he offers you a canteen on a hot dusty hike." He pointed out that those with segregationist views generally kept to themselves and friendships in uniform formed along economic, social, and educational lines rather than by race. But he felt that inequality outside the post was the prime source of a Negro soldier's frustration, "I'd rather be a private in Fort Lewis, Washington, than a general in Georgia."[11]

Both Lawrence and Moskos well reflect the newly gained economic and status advantages that military life had over civilian life for the colored soldier. These benefits encouraged more Negroes to join, to stay in, and even to publicly praise the better opportunities in the service.

Only Adam C. Powell, Harlem's Congressman, found it politically expedient to attack the military during the 1950's. For the most part, his comments, while often colorful, achieved only minor changes and had little impact on the larger issues of the Negro-military relationship that arose in the 1950's. On July 3, 1953, he attacked the personnel-assignment policy of the services as unfair; on March 31, 1954, he demanded abolition of the segregated mess detachment at West Point; on May 4, 1955, he unsuccessfully attempted to amend the Reserve Forces Act to abolish segregated Negro Reserve units. [12]

One reason for Powell's criticisms can be found in the nature of his Harlem constituency. As James Q. Wilson points out, Powell's re-election depends on a distribution of "ideal or nonmaterial" benefits, for his New York constituency has a "short supply of tangible patronage."[13] This requires Powell to make issues in order to gain the voters' attention, and to win their loyalty he attacks discriminatory practices, no matter how minor, in the Defense Department. But Representative William L. Dawson of Chicago has remained silent on Negro problems in the armed forces. As Professor Wilson explains, Dawson's district is different.

A strong political machine operates there to distribute ample tangible rewards for the faithful. Dawson, unlike Powell, does not need to encourage loyalties by publicizing military inequities.

Ironically, while Negro protest over the military was declining, Negro violence increased sharply in almost every other sector of America after the Korean War. A New York Times journalist, Anthony Lewis, has termed 1954 to 1964 "the revolutionary decade,"[14] for during this period active Negro dissent was concerned with desegregation of lunch counters, schools, housing, buses, and jobs. The prime reason for a decline in protest over the armed services and its rise elsewhere was that the Negroes had obtained their major goals from the military but not from general society.

Short-Run Unit Dislocation, Long-Run Structural Improvement for the Defense Establishment

Reclassification of 250,000 men into different units produced a considerable change in the military establishment, but the dislocation was eased in three ways. First, the change did not occur all at once. The Air Force integrated in 1949, the Army in Korea integrated in the spring and summer of 1951, and the European and American continental forces early in 1952. Second, the reforms took place during a high influx of personnel. Drafting up to twenty times as many men during the Korean War as at its start rapidly increased the number of newly formed units and made it easier to reassign Negroes. Third, only one unit actually engaged in combat, the 24th Infantry, was eliminated. Thus, the major short-term dislocation took place in Europe and America, far removed from live combat.

In the long run, the defense establishment improved its operational efficiency through the change. First, there was a reduction in the areas of tension in the military. Segregation into all-Negro units had caused deep personal dissatisfaction to the men assigned to them. The men's feeling that they were discriminated against and treated unfairly contributed to poorer performance in combat and racial tensions in peacetime assignments. This is evidenced by the rare eruption of post race riots since Korea, whereas conflicts broke out monthly between white and Negro units in World War II at most bases having black and white troops.

A riot did explode on March 24, 1960, at West Mesa Air Force Station near Albuquerque, New Mexico. It was considered an outbreak between Negro and white soldiers until an investigation revealed it was merely a fight over a girl following a dance. As Civil Rights Counselor James Evans emphasizes, "no torrid" incidents have happened that can be attributed to integration. [15]

Nor, since Korea, have commanders hesitated to commit units to combat because they were not sure how well Negroes would react under fire. As one brigadier general concisely stated: "No question about it--mix 'em up and you get a stronger line all the way. Segregate 'em and you have a point of weakness in your line where the enemy will surely attack. "[16]

Besides fewer riots and a stronger line, the armed services, like any other large human organization, require many talents to make them run. Several thousand different categories of skills are essential. It is easier to keep the organization going if human beings with a particular skill can readily be trained and transferred, like interchangeable parts on a car, to a neighboring unit or geographic area requiring those talents. Similarly, manpower is wasted if too many of the same skills must be confined to one area. Segregation is an irrational force that prevents efficient allocation of human resources. As the final report of the Fahy Committee emphasized: "Segregation forced inefficiency in two ways. By requiring skilled Negroes to serve in racial units, the Army often lost the skills for which these individuals had been trained. On the other hand, by concentrating large numbers in noncombat units the military multiplied inefficiency a second way. "[17] In short, for a military organization wanting to do a job the swiftest and easiest way integration was more effective in educating and then allocating human resources.

Finally, integration brought the military organization improved support from the Negro community and, an increased colored commitment to filling military needs. Defense budgets as well as draft laws encountered less opposition from Negroes after 1953 than in 1948. Recruitment had greater incentive for the Negro, who was offered equal treatment in uniform. Good publicity of the new reforms boosted the Defense Department's prestige in colored and white circles alike, thus reaping the indirect benefit of added political support.

General Support of Military Leadership
for the Integration Program

Retired General Mark Clark caused an uproar on April 28, 1956, when in a public address he stated: "My World War II experience persuaded me that Negro units in combat tended to be undependable under fire."[18] But Clark was addressing a Conference of the Council of State Government in Charleston, South Carolina, and was then commandant of the oldest, most distinguished military academy in the South, the Citadel. He was telling his conservative Southern audience what they expected to hear.

Nonetheless, Clark concluded that groupments of Negroes were a weakness for the military organization:

> Since we have Negroes in our Army, and since they demonstrably cannot or will not fight effectively as all-Negro units, there is really no choice, if they are to share fairly in the burden of the conflict, except to insert a small percentage of them into white units. [19]

Clark had long been immersed in the Army's racial policy and its fears about what would happen if integration took place, both while Fifth Army Commander in Italy (where the 92nd Division was under his command) and United Nations Commander during the Korean conflict. But now his profession demanded that he accept the reform for many good reasons. He did and recognized its practicality, but his speech shows how difficult it was for at least one Army leader to switch moral positions so rapidly.

In contrast to Clark, retired Major General Anthony McAuliffe reflected the practical attitudes that military leaders were now putting forth as the rewards of integration in the Army: "I should say that the integration of the Negro in the Armed Forces has worked very well and that we are getting much greater usefulness from the available manpower than we ever did under segregation. We didn't do it to improve the social situation. It was merely a matter of getting the best out of the military personnel that was available."[20]

Like McAuliffe, most officers were realistic and pragmatic. They understood that integration made for a more

efficient defense organization. Not for the Negro but for the
organization, the change was a good thing. Even if the officer
disagreed, professional responsibility prevented him from
speaking out against the new policy. He took reform in stride,
like any other order. No officer has ever been reported to
have resigned because of integration. Moreover, compelling
personal motivations often caused officers to favor it. For
example, officers who had been assigned to command all-
Negro units often found this an obstacle in developing their
careers. [21] For the most part, both military and career considerations made professional soldiers just as glad as the Negroes to see the all-colored units go.

Limited Influence Upon Nonmilitary Life

Outside the military sphere, integration of the armed
forces caused little appreciable change in the pattern of American life. Kenneth Clark, a Kansas liberal, used the military
example to support his writings for school desegregation that
were used in the Supreme Court case that produced the Brown
Decision (1953). [22] Thomas Pettigrew, a Harvard University
sociologist, points out that Southern white veterans tend to be
more tolerant of Negroes than Southern white males without
military service. But this, he adds, might just as well be due
to the cosmopolitan influence of the services as to any direct
contact there with Negro soldiers. [23]

There was no report of a town integrating its facilities
after a nearby base integrated. Nor were there reports of
individuals who went into the service as segregationists and
returned home to integrate the community. When men returned to civilian life, they returned to the prejudices, attitudes, and beliefs of their locale. Mark Clark is an example
of an officer who, upon coming back to civilian life, resumed
his society's habits.

In short, military influence extended about as far as the
post gate. In 1953, military integration had made little if
any direct impact upon the values of the neighboring communities, which were supported by their own peculiar set of
political forces.

THE AMORPHOUS AREAS

"Amorphous" was the label given to certain issues by a panel established under President Kennedy to investigate the problems of the Negro-military relationship in 1962. These issues tend to be in a twilight zone, outside the direct influence of the military organization and beyond the reach of the Negro community's political pressure. Untouched by the direct powers of either group, these areas have been under considerable control by the forces of exclusion during the 1950's and 1960's. Since there are no easy solutions to the resulting problems, these amorphous areas will no doubt be troublesome for some time to come. They fall into three broad categories: 1) distribution; 2) local segregation; and 3) the National Guard.

The Problem of Distribution

In an Army Register article in 1959, the longtime Pentagon civil-rights counselor James C. Evans expressed the thought that "refinement," not "segregation" nor "discrimination," was the chief concern of the armed-forces civil-rights counsel.[24] "Refinement," he implied, meant the achievement of a more equitable distribution of Negroes throughout the service. Too few generals, officers, senior NCO's, and skilled NCO's are Negroes. There are too many Negroes in lower-grade, enlisted positions, particularly nonskilled jobs.

Generally, statistics place the military profession in a very favorable position. As of 1965, while 11 per cent of the American population was Negro, 8.2 per cent of the military was colored.[25] The average profession was 1.5 per cent Negro, the officer corps 1.6 per cent.[26] From 1949 to 1964, the services increased their percentages of Negroes in enlisted ranks from 4.7 to 5.8 per cent for the Navy; 5.1 to 10.0 per cent for the Air Force; 2.1 to 8.7 per cent for the Marines; and 12.4 to 13.4 per cent for the Army. Officer percentages also went up during that period: the Navy from 0 to .3 per cent; the Marines from 0 to .4 per cent; the Air Force from .6 to 1.5 per cent; and the Army from 1.8 per cent to 3.4 per cent (see Table 2). From 1953 to 1965, the percentage of inductions and enlistments of Negro NCO's into the individual services rose: the Army from 14.7 to 16.3 per cent (inducted) and from 13.4 to 14.1 per cent (enlisted); the Navy from 4.3

TABLE 2

Trend Toward Higher Percentages of Negroes (Enlisted Men/Officers)
in Armed Forces over Selective Years, 1949-64

| | Army | | Navy | | Marine Corps | | Air Force | | Total Per Cent in Defense Department |
	Enlisted Men	Officers	Enlisted Men	Officers	Enlisted Men	Officers	Enlisted Men	Officers	
1949	12.4	1.8	4.7	0	2.1	0	5.1	.6	N.A.
1954	13.7	3.0	3.6	.1	6.6	.1	8.6	1.1	N.A.
1962	12.2	3.2	5.2	.2	7.6	.2	9.2	1.2	N.A.
1964	13.4	3.4	5.8	.3	8.7	.4	10.0	1.5	11.7

Note: The percentage of Negroes in the U.S. population is 11.4 (1964) and the percentage of Negroes in the U.S. Government is 13.1 (1964).

Source: Unpublished data obtained from Civil Rights Office, Department of Defense.

to 5.8 per cent; the Marines from 8.0 to 8.4 per cent; and
the Air Force from 11.1 to 13.1 per cent. These figures reflect the increasing acceptance of the Negro in all branches
of the armed forces and a limited breakthrough into the officer ranks. (See Table 3.)

While this rise has not been steady, it indicates that Negroes have a strong interest in joining the services. The
draft is not the only factor that is bringing them into the military, since the difference between the Army's draft rate and
voluntary enlistment rate is not that significant. Thus, the
threat of being drafted could not be considered as a cause for
the increased Negro interest. Furthermore, these figures
show that the Navy's image in Negro eyes is still not very
good, compared to the Army and Air Force, but at least
its statistics are improving. The best indicator that Negroes
like what the services offer them is their first-term re-
enlistment rates, which, in 1964, for each service averaged
twice as high for Negroes as the whites. (See Table 4.)

The pattern of distribution within the defense organization presents a less favorable picture. In the Army, Navy,
Air Force, and Marines, the percentages and numbers of Negro officers in 1962 (see Table 5) revealed few in senior grades,
and the bulk as lieutenants and captains. There is only one
general, the Air Force's Lieutenant General Benjamin O.
Davis, Jr. The highest-ranking officers for the Army are six
colonels, and only in March, 1966, did the Navy appoint its
first Negro captain, Thomas D. Parham, a chaplain.[27]

A prime means of increasing the numbers of professional
Negro officers is the service academies. There are 9,800 cadets at these schools (3,000 at West Point, 4,000 at Annapolis,
and 2,800 at the Air Force Academy), but in March, 1966,
there were only 52 Negro cadets or .5 per cent of the students
in these schools (U.S.M.A. has 28, U.S.N.A. has 9, and
U.S.A.F. has 15). (See Table 6.) Eleven Negroes graduated
in June, 1965, from these schools--one eighth of all Negroes
who have graduated from these schools since 1887 (86 colored
graduates have been commissioned from the academies since
1887). While the number of Negroes graduating each year is
slowly increasing, Table 6 illustrates the small percentage of
Negroes in the student bodies compared to the 11-per-cent
Negro population in the American population.

TABLE 3

Percentage of Inductions and Enlistments of Negroes
into Services over Selected Years, 1953-65

	Army		Navy	Marine Corps	Air Force
	Inducted	Enlisted			
1953	14. 7	13. 4	4. 3	8. 0	11. 1
1958	13. 2	6. 4	2. 8	5. 1	7. 1
1962	15. 3	9. 0	4. 1	6. 5	8. 6
1965	16. 3	14. 1	5. 8	8. 4	13. 1

Source: Unpublished data obtained from Civil Rights Office,
Department of Defense.

TABLE 4

First-Term Re-enlistment Rates of Negroes and
Whites by Service and Percentage, 1964

Service	White	Negro
Army	18. 5	49. 3
Navy	21. 6	41. 3
Marine Corps	12. 9	25. 1
Air Force	27. 4	50. 3

Source: Unpublished data obtained from Civil Rights Office, Department of Defense.

TABLE 5

Number and Percentage of Negro Personnel in Each Officer Rank, 1962

Rank		Service			
Navy	Army, Air Force and Marine Corps	Army	Navy	Air Force	Marine Corps
Admirals (all types)	Generals (all types)	0(0%)	0(0%)	1(0.29%)	0(0%)
Captains	Colonels	6(0.11%)	0(0%)	6(0.14%)	0(0%)
Commanders	Lt. Colonels	117(0.95%)	3(0.03%)	67(2.54%)	0(0%)
Lt. Commanders	Majors	424(2.47%)	17(0.14%)	124(0.60%)	0(0%)
Lieutenants	Captains	1,532(5.21%)	88(0.35%)	615(1.74%)	7(0.17%)
Lieutenants (j.g.)	1st Lieutenants	650(4.33%)	57(0.39%)	317(1.56%)	16(0.44%)
Ensigns	2nd Lieutenants	421(2.26%)	29(0.22%)	170(1.45%)	9(0.28%)
Total Officers and Percentages		3,150(3.2%)	194(0.26%)	1,300(1.24%)	32(0.21%)

Note: 1962 Data for all Services. The Air Force figures include only officers assigned to duty in the 48 States of the continental United States. All other figures are complete and world-wide in scope.

Source: Gesell Committee Initial Report, June 13, 1963, p. 10.

67

TABLE 6

Negro Graduates of West Point, Annapolis, and the Air Force Academy, 1877-1965

West Point (Established 1802)		Annapolis (Established 1845)		Air Force Academy (Established 1954)	
Date	Number of Negroes	Date	Number of Negroes	Date	Number of Negroes
1877	1	1949	1	1963	3
1887	1	1952	1	1964	1
1889	1	1953	1	1965	4
1936	1	1954	1		
1941	1	1955	1		
1943	2	1956	2		
1944	1	1957	2		
1945	2	1958	1		
1946	1	1959	4		
1949	2	1961	3		
1950	2	1962	2		
1951	5	1963	1		
1953	3	1964	4		
1954	3	1965	3		
1955	5				
1956	1				
1957	2				
1958	1				
1959	2				
1960	1				
1961	2				
1962	1				
1963	4				
1964	2				
1965	4				

TABLE 6 - Continued

Negro Graduates of West Point, Annapolis, and the Air
Force Academy, 1877-1965

Total
Graduates:

51(West Point)   27(Annapolis)   8(Air Force
                                                      Academy)

Currently
Enrolled:

28(West Point)   9(Annapolis)   15(Air Force
                                                      Academy)

Total Number of Academy
Students:

3,000(West Point)   4,000(Annapolis)   2,800(Air Force
                                                      Academy)

Percentage of Negroes in
Academy Student Body:

.9%(West Point)   .2%(Annapolis)   .5%(Air Force
                                                      Academy)

Note: As a comparison, representation at Ivy League univer-
       sities is not much higher. Harvard's class of '69 has
       27 Negroes out of 1,205, or 2.2 per cent, of the fresh-
       man class.

Source: Unpublished data obtained from Civil Rights Of-
         fice, Department of Defense.

The chief source of Negro officers entering the services is the R. O. T. C. at Negro colleges. At the fifteen predominantly Negro schools, in 1964-65, the Army R. O. T. C. had 7, 622 cadets (a gain of 353 cadets over the year before) and the Air Force R. O. T. C. had 3, 106 (a gain of 406). There are no Navy R. O. T. C. 's at these colleges, and so this service is deprived of an important avenue of minority recruitment. [28]

As in the officer ranks, there is also a noticeably uneven distribution of Negroes in enlisted grades. The percentages and numbers of top-ranking E-9 (top sergeants) Negroes in the Army, Navy, Air Force, and Marine Corps are significantly lower than in the E-1 (private) or E-5 (lowest sergeant) range. (See Table 7.) In enlisted job occupations, Negroes are concentrated heavily in unskilled or semiskilled occupations. Table 8 notes their heavy concentration in the infantry, the Navy's food service, as medical and dental assistants, and in service and supply work (truck drivers and quartermaster). Fewer are in the growing skill fields of electronics, communications, and mechanical repair. Nevertheless, the Navy made a remarkable reform from World War II,when 100 per cent of its Negroes were in the stewards' branch, to twenty years later, when only 11 per cent of this category is colored. Table 9 reflects how small the professional skilled Negro class is in the military and how the skill distribution of Negro officers in the military compares to Negro professional employment in the civilian world. At the professional level, there seems to be a close relation between armed-forces and civilian distribution. In some fields--legal, medical, and the clergy--the armed-forces percentages are below those for civilian employment, but in others--engineering, air pilots, and finance--the military has better representation.

In sum, the distribution of the Negroes in the services compared to that of whites shows less involvement in leadership and skilled roles and greater participation in support, nonskilled, and subordinate employment in enlisted and officer ranks. Of the three services, the Navy in twenty years has made the greatest change, but still, in comparison with the Army and Air Force, has a poorer capability of attracting Negroes into its ranks.

TABLE 7

Number and Percentage of Negro Personnel in Each Enlisted Grade, 1962

Grade	Army	Navy	Air Force	Marine Corps
E-9 (highest)	76(2.97%)	22(1.30%)	32(0.83%)	5(0.71%)
E-8	586(5.72%)	89(1.22%)	140(1.67%)	19(0.81%)
E-7	3,143(7.64%)	984(2.42%)	616(2.51%)	142(2.12%)
E-6	10,496(12.65%)	2,843(4.43%)	2,115(4.19%)	417(3.93%)
E-5	21,892(16.28%)	5,370(6.23%)	10,287(9.33%)	1,490(8.65%)
E-4	21,133(12.20%)	6,771(6.59%)	14,321(12.47%)	2,663(9.08%)
E-3	26,385(11.90%)	7,502(5.11%)	11,505(9.26%)	3,101(8.14%)
E-2	10,836(10.58%)	5,396(5.22%)	6,951(10.23%)	3,727(8.01%)
E-1 (lowest)	8,456(11.15%)	1,431(4.77%)	597(17.17%)	1,787(7.55%)
Total Enlisted Members and Percentages	103,003(12.14%)	30,408(5.22%)	46,564(9.1%)	13,351(7.59%)

Note: The Air Force figures are drawn from certain selected commands and represent about 76 per cent of all Air Force enlisted personnel. All other figures are complete and worldwide in scope.

Source: Gesell Committee Initial Report, June 13, 1963, p. 9.

TABLE 8

Occupational-Group Distribution by Race--Percentage
of Negroes in Each Occupation, 1965

Infantry	16. 4%	Administrative and Clerical	10. 3%
Electronic Equipment Repairment	5. 5%	Technical and Mechanical Equipment Repairment	7. 1%
Communications and Intelligence	6. 7%	Craftsmen	9. 3%
Medical and Dental	11. 8%	Service and Supply	16. 9%
Other Technical and Allied	7. 8%	Navy's Food Service	13. 0%

Source: Unpublished data obtained from Civil Rights Office,
Department of Defense.

TABLE 9

Percentage of Negro Officers in Armed Forces' Professional Occupational Groupings

	Male Civilian Employment, 1960	Armed Forces, 1962				
		Total	Army	Air Force	Navy	Marines
		Professional and managerial versus military officers				
1. Legal	1.0	0.7	1.0	0.8	..	N.A.
2. Chemical and scientific	2.0	2.8	5.1	1.7	..	..
3. Electrical engineers, signal, electronics, etc.	0.7	2.2	3.1	1.8	0.1	0.2
4. Civil, aeronautical, and other engineers	0.6	1.4	2.6	1.0	0.0	..
5. Finance, accountants, auditors, etc.	0.9	1.5	1.8	1.4	N.A.	0.5
6. Supply, transportation, and misc. managers	0.9	2.2	3.8	1.6	0.1	0.4
7. Physicians, medical corps	2.0	1.2	1.7	1.2	0.6	N.A.
8. Dentists	2.5	1.6	1.9	2.4	0.4	N.A.
9. Nurses	5.4	3.4	3.8	4.5	1.3	N.A.
10. Clergymen, chaplains	7.1	1.9	3.2	1.6	0.4	N.A.
11. Air pilots and navigators	0.4	0.7	N.A.	0.4	0.2	0.2
12. Policemen, etc.; officers in military police, etc.	3.4	3.2	3.7	1.8	N.A.	..

Source: John P. Davis, ed., American Negro Reference Book (Englewood Cliffs, N.J.: Prentice-Hall, 1966), p. 229.

The imbalanced colored distribution within the defense organization prevails because of four significant forces: 1) the Negro class structure; 2) the increasing shift from nonskilled to skilled roles within the services; 3) the higher professional competition for Negro college graduates; and 4) the rising expectations of militant Negro demands for social respect.

Colored roles within the armed services reflect the civilian world, in which there is a small, educated, professional middle class and a sizable, uneducated lower class. Negro talent is simply in short supply: 26.1 per cent of common laborers are Negro and only 0.9 per cent of accountants, 0.7 per cent of electrical engineers and 1.0 per cent of lawyers are Negro. [29] In 1964, while 8.1 per cent of whites had acquired a college education, 3.5 per cent of Negroes were college graduates; yet, in that same year, when 3.4 per cent of whites remained unemployed, 9.8 per cent of Negroes were out of work. [30] Thus, the professional needs of the military, plus the shortage of Negro talent cause the unbalanced distribution within the services. (See Table 10 for President Kennedy's 1963 statistics on the differing social structures of the white and Negro communities.)

Second, technological change has rocked the military establishment since World War II. All figures show a rapidly increased percentage of skilled jobs and a decreased percentage of ground combat forces. From 1945 to 1958, the percentage of technicians (electronics and mechanics experts) increased from 34.4 per cent to 46.7 per cent, and the ground combat forces declined from 23.6 per cent to 12.9 per cent. [31] Table 11 reflects the immense change in our military organization caused by automation from the Civil War to the present. Note how within one hundred years, technical and scientific personnel have increased from .2 to 14.5 per cent, and military and combat jobs have declined from 93.2 to 28.8 per cent. Table 12 breaks down by service the needs of each for skilled individuals. This table gives some idea of why integration took place faster in the Air Force and more slowly in the Navy. The Air Force had technically skilled Negro manpower, and its segregated Negroes could be shifted more rapidly into other skilled roles. Although the Navy lists 46.3 per cent of its personnel in combat status, the men serving aboard ships are highly skilled. Thus, the Navy, having a predominantly

TABLE 10a

Differing Social Structures of White and Black Communities

AS THE PRESIDENT DESCRIBED IT

The Negro has "twice as much chance of becoming unemployed..."

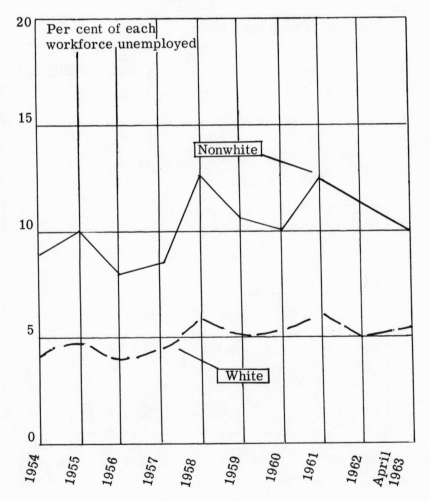

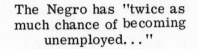

TABLE 10b

Differing Social Structures of White and Black Communities

AS THE PRESIDENT DESCRIBED IT

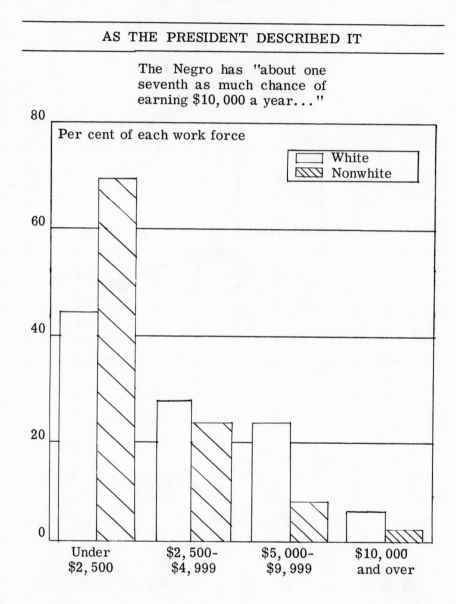

The Negro has "about one seventh as much chance of earning $10,000 a year..."

Per cent of each work force

White
Nonwhite

Under $2,500 $2,500-$4,999 $5,000-$9,999 $10,000 and over

TABLE 10c

Differing Social Structures of White and Black Communities

STATUS OF THE NEGRO IN THE U.S. TODAY

The Negro has "about one half
as much chance of completing
high school..."

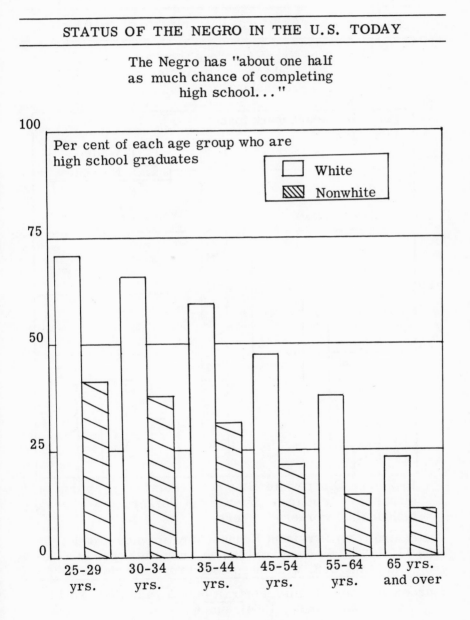

Per cent of each age group who are
high school graduates

☐ White
▧ Nonwhite

| | 25-29 yrs. | 30-34 yrs. | 35-44 yrs. | 45-54 yrs. | 55-64 yrs. | 65 yrs. and over |

TABLE 10d

Differing Social Structures of White and Black Communities

STATUS OF THE NEGRO IN THE U.S. TODAY

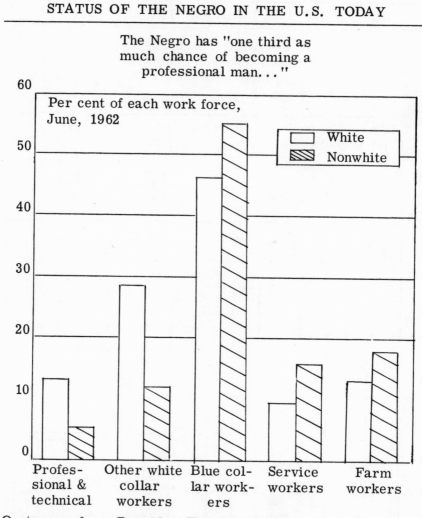

The Negro has "one third as much chance of becoming a professional man..."

Per cent of each work force, June, 1962

☐ White
▨ Nonwhite

Profes-
sional &
technical

Other white
collar
workers

Blue col-
lar work-
ers

Service
workers

Farm
workers

Quotes are from President Kennedy's nationwide broadcast, June 11, 1963. He compared the opportunities open to a Negro child in the U.S. with those open to a white child.

Source: Anthony Lewis, Portrait of a Decade (New York: Random House, 1964), pp. 6 and 7.

TABLE 11

Trend Toward Larger Needs for Technical Manpower in the
Military and Fewer Purely Military Specialists
(Percentages)

Occupational Group	Civil War	Spanish-American War	World War I	World War II	Korea	1954
Technical-Scientific	.2	.5	3.7	10.1	10.7	14.5
Administrative-Clerical	.7	3.1	8.0	14.6	19.2	17.5
Skilled Mechanics	.6	1.1	21.5	15.8	16.9	20.3
Service Workers	2.4	6.5	12.5	9.7	11.5	10.4
Laborers	2.9	2.2	20.2	13.6	8.6	8.4
Military-Combat Type	93.2	86.6	34.1	36.2	33.1	28.8

Source: Morris Janowitz, The Professional Soldier (New York: Free Press, 1960), p. 65.

79

TABLE 12

Differing Service Needs for Technical Manpower,
by Percentages, 1954

Occupational Group	Marines	Army	Navy	Air Force
Technical-Scientific	8.9	14.5	13.4	21.7
Administrative-Clerical	18.9	17.4	8.0	23.7
Skilled Mechanics	17.4	12.5	22.2	24.5
Service Workers	6.2	10.4	6.4	20.7
Laborers	7.2	8.4	0	4.6
Military-Combat Type	35.8	28.8	46.3	0

Source: Morris Janowitz, The New Military (New York: Russell Sage Foundation, 1964), p. 43.

unskilled group of Negro messmen through World War II, had difficulty in transferring them quickly into other assignments.

Another indicator of the military's increasing technical needs is the rising educational level of the services. (See Table 13.) In 1961, 75 per cent of the officers were college graduates and 99.8 per cent had a high-school diploma. Even among enlisted personnel, 73 per cent had graduated from high school. In 1942, the armed forces had only two ratings in the radar and fire control field; in 1958, there were twenty-seven such ratings. Seventy-two previously nonexistent positions in guided missiles, and nine in atomic weapons became available.[32] Like other organizations within America, the military is becoming more specialized, educated, and automated. Due to technical change, the Negro, whose primary role in the military has been in less skilled, nonmanagerial jobs, will find decreasing opportunities for unskilled employment in the services. Presently, his position seems secure because of the manpower needs created by the Vietnam conflict, but a peaceful settlement and a decline in military strength would sizably decrease the demand for the majority of untrained Negroes in the defense establishment.

A third pressure limits the number of talented Negroes that the military can obtain. Outside demands discourage young Negroes from entering the armed services. In the typical middle-class home in 1955, parents ranked the military seventh among the professions that they wished to see their sons follow--behind law, medicine, and business.[33] Not only the home but aggressive recruiting by other fields pulls the limited numbers of Negro college graduates away from the armed forces. A February 6, 1966, New York Times article pointed out:

> The drive to recruit qualified Negro candidates for employment in business and industry has led to publication of "Opportunities for the College Grad" by Richard and Clarke Associates...All of its 13 full-page ads, which will appear only in this publication, in essence bear the same message: "We are interested in considering you for employment." Short articles, in addition to ads by various business firms, brief the job-seeker on the practical matters of writing the resumé

TABLE 13

Trend Toward Higher Educational Level in the Military,
in Percentages, 1944-61

Educational Level	1944		1952		1961	
	Enlisted Men	Officers	Enlisted Men	Officers	Enlisted Men	Officers
College Graduate	1	34	4	50	2	75
Any College	11	67	14	76	18	97
High School Graduate	41	82	48	97	73	99.8
Any High School	70	99.8	76	99.8	96	99.8

Source: Morris Janowitz, The New Military (New York: Russell Sage Foundation, 1964), p. 54.

and letter of application, the technique of the
interview, and "How to use your College
Placement Office. "[34]

Daniel Patrick Moynihan wrote in the 1965 Fall Daedalus:

> Anyone with eyes to see can observe the emergence
> of a Negro middle class that is on the whole doing
> very well. This group has, if anything, rather a
> preferred position in the job market. A nation
> catching up with centuries of discrimination has
> rather sharply raised the demand for a group in
> short supply. One would be hard put to describe
> a person with better job opportunities than a newly
> minted Negro Ph. D. [35]

Thus, the armed services are competing with other
American organizations for a limited group. With smaller
monetary incentives, the services will find it increasingly difficult to hold onto a group of individuals in great demand by
the business world.

Moreover, the armed services are confronted with a
fourth pressure: the rising expectations of a militant Negro
community. Riots in urban centers like Watts in Los Angeles
express the Negro's frustrations. Although he has more material benefits today, he expects much more from the future.
If the services fail to respond to his hopes, they can become
the object of intense political pressure, as in 1948. The military's present racial picture is good only because it contrasts
so sharply with the Negro's plight in the rest of America. A
continued imbalance in distribution could invoke renewed Negro
criticism. A preview of this appeared in the January, 1966,
issue of Ebony:

> Of all areas of American life, the military often
> claims to be the least bigoted. Yet Negroes above
> the grade of junior officer are rare birds, whether
> in the Army, Navy, Air Force or Marine Corps. [36]

James Farmer, national director of CORE, in a New
York Times interview on January 3, 1966, called the military
a "splendid example of American tokenism. "[37] Singling out
the Navy's record, he stated:

Of course, the Navy has a notoriously ugly
history concerning the advancement of Negro
commissioned personnel. What is important
is that neither the Navy nor the Marine Corps
can point to a single Negro line officer in the
grades of Captain, Colonel or above.

It would be wise for Navy selection boards
to consult their opposite numbers in the other
services to learn what the 20th century is
about. [38]

What should be done about this critical manpower distribution problem in light of these pressures? This important
question should be of central concern to several high Pentagon
administrators--political as well as military--before the situation reaches unmanageable dimensions. There are two avenues open within the defense structure to rectify the dilemma:
1) wider Negro availability to officer-training programs, and
2) careful counseling of Negro officer career patterns.

First, simply using more recruiting posters with Negroes in officer uniforms will not bring many Negroes into the
services. The Negro professional class is small and in high
demand. Thus, to compete favorably, the armed forces must
offer greater tangible organizational inducements for them to
join and stay in. Easier access to the three modes of entry--
academies, Reserve Officer Training, and officer candidate
schools--could be the greater incentive Negroes need.

More than four fifths of appointments to the service
academies are controlled by individual Congressmen. [39] As in
the past, the election of more Negro Congressmen will boost
the numbers of Negroes appointed. Increased Negro Congressional strength has been the greatest single source of more
Negro appointments to the armed-services academies. The
election of Southern Republican Negro Congressmen during the
Reconstruction brought the first Negro youths to West Point.
The election of DePriest in Chicago in 1929 gave General
Benjamin O. Davis, Jr., his appointment. Today both Congressmen Powell and Dawson supply a continuous stream of
Negroes for the academies. [40]

But the election of more Negro Congressmen will take
time, so another method of getting more Negroes into West

Point, Annapolis, and the Air Force Academy ought to be considered. Often, for want of qualified Congressional candidates, appointments are turned over for the academies' own choice. Many of these appointments go to athletes to improve the school's sports teams. The service schools ought to be encouraged to make a greater effort to find qualified Negro youngsters for these vacancies.

Reserve Officer Training is another way to enter the officer ranks, and although it is less career-oriented, Reserve officers account for two fifths of the profession. [41] Two improvements could increase Negro involvement in the R.O.T.C. First, there are no N.R.O.T.C. units at Negro colleges. Establishing such units at predominantly colored colleges would open the door for far more Negro officers in the Navy. Second, perhaps it would be in the national interest for Congress to consider establishing an eleventh and twelfth grade preparatory school for bright but underprivileged youths who desire to attend either a service academy or a university with an N.R.O.T.C. but lack the education to be admitted. Training at such a prep school could supply the education these youngsters need in order to compete favorably for positions in academies or universities with those from more fortunate backgrounds. Such a school could develop the human potential of the poor by stimulating their education as well as offering them an avenue into a military profession.

Officer Candidate Schools in each branch of the armed forces turn out a competent, dedicated, but often less-educated officer. These schools offer the noncommissioned officer a chance to become a commissioned officer by passing a rigorous three months of schooling. While the standards are high, it would not lower them to encourage more Negroes to apply and attend, and there are many colored soldiers in the range from E-5 to E-2 (see Table 7) who would probably do well as officers but need the stimulation to try for O.C.S. The Pentagon could encourage these schools to increase Negro attendance in O.C.S., which might prod military educators at these schools to look more carefully for able Negroes who could become suitable officers.

Second, inadequate career patterns promote imbalanced distribution of nonwhites in the military. Promotion boards study not the officer's picture but the pattern of his career. Reviewing officers, except in specialties of supporting arms

like medicine, expect a certain amount of the person's time
to be spent in troop command, education, and overseas staff
duty.   Presently, any officer, Negro or white, faces severe
competition for promotion in grades above major due to the
World War II "hump" of officers still on active duty.[42] If
a Negro is going to compete favorably with his able white contemporaries, he must be encouraged to develop a background
with the characteristics that promotion boards are looking for.
Staff assignments, troop leadership, and education have been
the primary qualities lacking in Negro officers.   The expanding
war in South Vietnam should open greater opportunities for
troop leadership.

But command experience is still small.   The senior
leadership posts that Negroes hold in the armed forces today
are: Lieutenant General Benjamin Davis--Chief of Staff, U.S.
Forces in Korea and U.N. Command in Seoul; Colonel Frederic
E. Davison--Brigade Commander, U.S. Army Training Center
at Fort Bliss, Texas; and in the Navy: Commander S.L.
Gravely--commander of the destroyer U.S.S. Falgout; Lieu-
tenant Commander G.I. Thompson--in charge of the U.S.S.
Finch; and Lieutenant Commander J.S. Lee--in charge of the
U.S.S. Aeolus, a cable-repair ship.[43]

Besides command experience, staff assignments still
seem to be a problem for Negro officers, as indicated by
Table 14 of Negroes assigned to the major Army and Air Force
command centers.   The Joint Chiefs of Staff, for example,
has been traditionally a place difficult for Negroes to obtain
positions.[44]

Table 15 illustrates how few colored men have graduated
from senior military educational institutions.   From these six
schools, only seven Negroes have graduated.   Davis was the
first Negro to attend the Air War College, from 1949 to 1950.
Colonel Davison was the first colored officer to enter the
Army War College in 1962.   Commander Gravely and Lieutenant Commander Thompson were at the Naval War College from
1964 to 1965.   Attending these schools is important not merely
for the education received there but also because it is here one
meets contemporaries who may sit on future promotion boards.
The social experience rather than the learning aspect makes
acceptance to these schools important for Negro military advancement.[45]

TABLE 14

Negro Officers Assigned to Major
Command Headquarters, 1965

Army Headquarters

OSD	2	USARYIS	1	USARE	0
DIA	6	USARL	2	EUCOM	0
DCA	1	JCS	0	USSOCMD	0
USARP	2	STRIKCOM	0		
USARJ	2	UNCOMD	0		

Air Command Centers

Alaskan	5	USAF Headquarters Command	5
Air Defense	34	JCS	15
Air Force Accounting	1	MATS	4
Air Communications Service	6	Office of Aerospace Research	2
Logistics	2	Pacific Air Force	8
Air Force Systems	4	SAC	7
Air Training Command	3	TAC	4
Air University	1	USAFA	1
Continental Air Command	2	USAF in Europe	22
NATO	2	USAF in Southern Europe	1
Korea	1		

Source: Unpublished information obtained from Civil Rights
Office, Department of Defense.

TABLE 15

Negro Graduates of Senior Service Schools

	1965-66 (to Graduate in June)	Total Graduates
Industrial College of the Armed Forces	0	1
National War College	1	1
Army War College	1	3
Naval War College	1	1
Air War College	2	1
NATO Defense College	0	0
Total.....	5	7

Source: Unpublished information obtained from Civil Rights
Office, Department of Defense.

The politics of promotion--developing the right career
pattern that superiors will want to promote--is a subtle art in
military circles that Negro officers ought to master if they
expect to advance to higher grades. A study of the career development of the highest-ranking Negro officer, Lieutenant
General Benjamin O. Davis, Jr., sheds some light on how an
ambitious young officer should shape his upward destiny. Undoubtedly, an experienced Davis, Sr., the first Negro brigadier general, passed on some valuable advice to Davis, Jr.
A West Point education provided a firm base of professional
competence and military respect and was an important source
of later career friendships. As a flyer during World War II
and leader of the 332nd Air Squadron, he secured a reputation
as a warrior, a record for leadership, and valued expertise
as a fighter pilot. After the war, his conscientious staff work
in Washington and his choosing to join the newly organized Air
Force earned him rapid promotions. In 1949, he went to the
Air War College. By the early 1950's, he had become a brigadier general commanding an Air Force fighter squadron in
Okinawa. The scarce supply of talented, qualified Negroes
helped to secure his present lieutenant generalship and Chief
of Staff position in Korea. Although interviewed frequently by
Negro magazines, Davis is not a racial reformer; he closely
plays his role as military manager, war hero, and professional
soldier. Thus, Davis identifies with the values of the military profession, rather than the Negro class. He possesses
the attributes of a talented organization man, holds closely to
the goals of white-middle-class America, with his handsome,
light-skinned features, a pretty wife, and an interest in golf
and bridge. In short, Davis is sensitive to the bureaucratic
demands of his profession and responds adroitly, thereby pro-
moting his career. [46]

In sum, it is not discrimination but redistribution--
moving Negroes into skilled, leadership roles--that is today
the central problem of the armed forces. The Negro class
structure, military automation, an increasing demand for Negro college graduates elsewhere, and the Negro's rising expectations of social status frustrate efforts to solve the problem. Wider availability of officer training and career-pattern
counseling offers avenues for improvement.

The Problem of Local Segregation

The most painful problem for the colored soldier is going outside the post gate. Accustomed to integrated policies within, he is jarred by the startling contrasts offered by outside civilian life. It is difficult for him to adjust to equality inside and inequality outside. And soldiers do have to leave the post, for bases cannot provide all worldly wants. At an average base, one half of the married personnel live off the post for lack of housing. [47] Few posts have their own schools. The children of most military men are sent to neighboring civilian school systems, which the Department of Defense reimburses. Furthermore, off-post shopping and recreational areas are important supplements to the limited offerings of the PX, commissary, and officer and NCO clubs.

In 1962, of 201 U.S. installations of the Army and 559 of the Navy that had a 100 or more personnel, a considerable percentage were surrounded by segregated civilian public facilities: 24 per cent of Army bases and 25 per cent of the Navy's had segregated schools near by; 34 per cent of Army bases and 43 per cent of Navy yards were next to segregated restaurants and bars; 31 per cent of Army and 40 per cent of Navy units' civilian theaters were not integrated. (See Tables 16 and 17.) While it is more difficult to assess the housing situation, of the 487,408 military families living off post, 181,635 live in quarters below service standards. According to a Presidential report, segregation is a primary reason why 74,250 families live in housing that is substandard because of the dwelling or inadequate size for the family unit; and why 27,284 must reside an excessive distance from the base; and why 80,101 pay costs that exceed the serviceman's quarters allowance. [48]

Local segregation has a broad influence upon the military because of 1) the character of the American social structure, 2) the geographic position of bases, and 3) the limitations of military post facilities and pay scales.

First, the American social structure is the major reason why Negroes find difficulty outside the post gate. As Daniel Patrick Moynihan has emphasized, when it came to the Negro, the American melting pot failed to melt the differences. [49]

TABLE 16

Segregation of Public Facilities in Communities Adjacent
to Military Installations, 1962

Types of Segregated Public Facility	Number of Surveyed Installations and Activities with such Segregated Facilities		Number of Personnel Stationed Where Facilities are Segregated		Percentages of Surveyed Installations and Activities with Segregated Facilities	
	Army	Navy	Army	Navy	Army	Navy
Public Schools	48	143	178,109	58,500	24%	25%
Restaurants and Bars	68	238	257,893	110,000	34%	43%
Theaters	63	223	232,301	105,000	31%	40%
Swimming Pools	19	226	178,201	102,000	9%	40%
Golf Courses	38	164	190,931	82,000	19%	29%
Beaches	10	203	123,502	90,000	5%	36%
Bowling Alleys	32	194	205,901	103,000	16%	35%
Libraries	10	49	130,179	28,000	5%	9%
Public Transportation	4	47	41,091	22,000	2%	8%
Hotels, Motels	12	252	205,618	141,000	6%	45%
Churches	23	163	127,402	70,000	11%	29%

Note: The Army survey for this table covered 201 installations and activities, while the Navy survey covered 559. Each installation and activity surveyed had 100 or more military personnel assigned to it.

Source: Gesell Committee Initial Report, June 13, 1963, p. 45.

TABLE 17

Segregated Public Schools Serving Children of Service Personnel, 1962

	Army	Navy	Marine Corps	Air Force
Number of installations or activities (with 100 or more assigned military personnel) in areas where public schools are segregated	48	143	4	53
Number of military personnel assigned to such installations and activities	178,109	58,500	47,956	159,691
Percentage of all service installations of this size in such segregated-school areas	20%	25%	5%	18%

Source: Gesell Committee Initial Report, June 13, 1963, p. 82.

Churches, a good indicator of where people live, reflect the degree of separation. Ninety per cent of them are all white or all colored. [50] Philip M. Hauser, after a careful study of where Negroes live, concluded:

> Between 1910 and 1960, the Negro has been
> redistributed from the South to the North and
> West, and from rural to urban and metro-
> politan areas; but within the urban and metro-
> politan complexes the Negro American has
> become and has remained much more highly
> segregated than was true of white immigrants
> who flocked to the cities before him. [51]

Second, the geographic locations of the installations exacerbate the dilemma. Forty per cent are located near Southern communities with a high degree of separation between white and nonwhite. Many of these Southern posts are important command and training facilities, which house more than half of the servicemen stationed in the continental limits, such as: Norfolk Naval Base, Virginia; Quantico Marine Base, Virginia; Fort Bragg, South Carolina; Fort Benning, Georgia; Pensacola Naval Air Station, Florida; Maxwell Air Base, Alabama; Fort Sam Houston, Texas; and Fort Knox, Kentucky. [52]

Third, military pay scales and on-post facilities encourage living in separate areas. If an average post can house only half the married troops assigned to it, a critical demand arises for housing in the nearby area. This raises the selling price or rents of local housing. The Negro captain or E-5--the one most likely to be required to live off post since his rank is often not high enough to obtain on-post housing, and the one who is at that period of life most likely raising a family--is least able to afford the higher prices in the better neighborhoods, closer to the base. [53] His salary and quarters allowance, compared to those of higher ranks, have less bargaining power in encouraging a real-estate dealer to find him a suitable home in an integrated neighborhood nearby.

Considering the local nature of segregation, what can the military do to remedy the situation?

The basic fact is that the military has neither the organizational goals nor the political resources to remedy such a complex and pervasive issue. At best, the Defense

Department must rely upon other government agencies for re-
lief.   Federal enforcement of the Brown Decision by the Supreme Court (1953), the Public Accommodations Law, Title
IV passed by Congress in 1964, the voting rights legislation
enacted in 1965, and the use of federal education funds to prod
school integration will all encourage ending segregation in
local communities and, subsequently, directly benefit military personnel living in these cities. [54]

Relocation of military bases out of the South has been
suggested by some authorities. [55] However, this would be a
considerable financial cost and create major military dislocation.   Realistically weighing the advantages of such a move
against the resulting evils, the defense establishment, particularly during the Vietnam war, would find few incentives for
making such a significant change.

Within the military organizations, the key improvement
would be the expansion of on-post facilities to make room for
all who desire to live on base as well as the enlargement of
their recreational and shopping areas.   An alternative is the
doubling of the quarters allowance for officers and enlisted
personnel living off base. [56] This would give better bargaining
power to those who have to find homes through local real-estate
agents.   Doubling pay would be a powerful incentive for gaining
large enough homes, homes near enough to the post, and ones
in integrated areas.

The defense establishment, if it expects to attract and
keep professionally capable Negroes, already in high demand
and short supply, will have to continue to be concerned with
the Negroes' standard of living.   Indeed, actions by other federal branches and agencies are securing a more favorable civilian life for the Negro serviceman.   Moreover, the Defense
Department has tried hard not to send men into regions where
they are unwelcome.   For example, in 1957 when the 2nd Ar-
mored Division returned from Germany to Fort Hood, Texas,
thirty-one Negro servicemen who had married white women were
transferred to assignments in areas where miscegenation was
allowed. [57]

Widespread local segregation remains a difficulty for
most Negro soldiers and, consequently, affects military capabilities.   The military establishment has several remedies
for coping with this problem, but they require decisive

leadership from the top of the military hierarchy, as well as
a realization of what the problems are and what solutions are
available.

The National Guard

The Army and Air National Guard operate under command of the fifty state Governors and the state adjutant generals (the District of Columbia has a Guard unit also), except
during a war or national emergency, when the President is
authorized to take control of these units. Normally, the Guard
is a state responsibility fulfilling state needs, as in a civic
disorder or natural disaster. However, the Guard's federal
responsibility is derived from several sources. Article 1 of
the Constitution gives Congress the power to help maintain a
strong militia. Presently, nine tenths of the funds for Guard
operations come from the Federal Treasury.[58] Also, the
Guard is necessary to the security of America, and the President has the option of calling it to active service. Guard units
fought as part of the armed forces in World War II and in
Korea.[59] Third, the National Guard is one way in which the
individual can complete his national military obligation. An
eighteen-year-old can, instead of serving two or three years
in the regular Army, Navy, or Air Force, satisfy his national
military obligation by going on active duty for six months in
the State Guard (plus five and a half years in the Reserves).[60]
Finally, Federal authority is derived from the dual oath that all
Guard members must take--to support the state constitution
and to support the Federal Constitution.[61]

The Guard has two branches: the Army National Guard
and the Air National Guard. The former has nearly 4,000
units, 370,269 men, 2,732 armories, 939 maintenance shops,
51 shop hangars, and for 1965 had a $468.5 million allocation
in the United States budget.[62] The Air Guard is smaller, with
75 units, 72,141 men, 180 bases, 3,500 rated pilots, and for
fiscal 1965 had a $319.3 million Federal allocation.[63]

Table 18 shows that as of February 1, 1964, 5,780 of
the 442,410 Air and Army Guardsmen--or 1.5 per cent of
Guard strength--were Negroes, whereas the national population has 11 per cent colored. Unlike the Regular military,
with high over-all Negro participation, the National Guard has
generally low participation (1.3 per cent), few officers (only
20 states report having Negro officers), proportionately fewer

TABLE 18

Number of Negroes in Army and Air National Guard by State, 1964

State	Army National Guard		Air National Guard	
	Total	Negro	Total	Negro
Alabama	14,860	0	1,940	2
Alaska	1,887	5	243	2
Arizona	2,749	49	725	0
Arkansas	7,619	3	1,226	1
California	20,709	539	4,311	58
Colorado	2,630	8	953	19
Connecticut	5,644	30	941	5
Delaware	3,244	105	768	3
District of Columbia	1,546	631	834	78
Florida	7,126	21	809	2
Georgia	7,889	2	2,540	2
Hawaii	3,716	3	1,254	2
Idaho	3,028	0	777	0
Illinois	10,260	668	2,135	4
Indiana	9,311	73	1,272	1
Iowa	7,675	4	1,662	2
Kansas	6,383	35	1,141	2
Kentucky	4,634	40	728	1
Louisiana	6,842	3	887	2
Maine	2,464	2	1,041	0
Maryland	5,861	345	956	5
Massachusetts	14,329	87	1,904	3
Michigan	9,082	139	1,805	20
Minnesota	9,632	12	2,043	4
Mississippi	10,006	1	1,425	1
Missouri	8,036	96	1,753	4
Montana	2,333	3	741	0
Nebraska	3,579	0	662	1
Nevada	1,560	28	1,074	0
New Hampshire	2,007	1	683	0
New Jersey	14,203	294	1,994	46
New Mexico	3,039	36	602	5

TABLE 18 - Continued

State	Army National Guard		Air National Guard	
	Total	Negro	Total	Negro
New York	25,205	681	4,012	49
North Carolina	10,600	80	953	1
North Dakota	2,572	0	810	0
Ohio	13,842	305	3,304	19
Oklahoma	8,441	219	1,772	5
Oregon	5,509	9	1,152	5
Pennsylvania	17,841	409	3,353	34
Rhode Island	2,712	12	747	6
South Carolina	9,083	1	832	5
South Dakota	3,555	0	790	0
Tennessee	10,087	94	2,643	6
Texas	15,205	146	2,514	2
Utah	4,368	5	1,026	0
Vermont	2,661	3	793	0
Virginia	7,137	5	557	0
Washington	5,340	43	1,461	11
West Virginia	2,711	74	1,112	2
Wisconsin	8,634	5	1,753	3
Wyoming	1,274	2	528	1
TOTALS	370,650	5,356 (1.45%)	71,941	424 (.59%)

Source: Baltimore Sun (March 31, 1965), p. 5.

men in the Air than Army Guard (.58 per cent compared with 1.44 per cent), numerically the smallest number in Southern states with the highest Negro populations and higher percentages in urban, Northern, industrial centers. (See Table 19.) The participation index (see Table 20--the ratio of percentage of Negroes in Guard divided by percentage of Negroes in the state population) demonstrates three groupments of states as to Negro Guard participation: Twelve of the first eighteen states are considered Northern, urban, industrial types; eleven of the last fourteen are classed as more rural, agricultural, and Southern; and thirteen out of the middle sixteen tend to be Northern or Western rural areas (three states have no Negroes in their Guard: Idaho, South Dakota, and North Dakota).

All Guard units have followed the Regular military on integration since 1948 by dropping restrictions on Negro participation. According to Major General Winston P. Wilson, head of the National Guard Bureau, as of December 1, 1964, no state legally excludes Negroes and all but three states have at least token numbers in their organization.[64] North Carolina, on April 2, 1963, was the last state to repeal an anti-Negro statute; it had read, "No organization of colored troops shall be permitted to be organized..." That year, North Carolina enrolled twenty-one Negroes in its Guard.[65] But with one-fourth of its population colored, North Carolina has less than 1 per cent nonwhites in its Guard. It has removed legal barriers and substituted token acceptance in order to ensure continued Federal funds. The same is true for the other nine Deep South states, which have more than one-half of America's Negroes, which receive more than one-fourth of the federal funds for Guard operations, yet have but a handful of Negroes participating in their local militia activities.[66]

Table 21 shows that of the 122,670 men in Air and Army Guard units in eleven southern states, 539 were nonwhite in 1965, or .004 per cent of the total manpower. This was a significant increase of 169 men over the previous year's total, but a sizable gap still persists between the Negro percentage in these states and the percentage in the Guards.

Any improvements in the Negro's position in the Guard is frustrated by the nature of the shared state-Federal responsibility over its activities. The state controls the day-to-day operation of the Guard. Moreover, many units within the

TABLE 19

Ranking of States by Percentage of Negroes Serving in Guard

State	Total No. of Negroes in Guard (1964)	Total Unit Strength (1964)	% of Negroes in Guard	% of Negroes in State Population (1960)
States with over 5 per cent:				
1 District of Columbia	709	2,380	29.3	53.9
2 Illinois	670	12,395	5.4	10.0
3 Maryland	350	6,847	5.1	10.7
States with between 5 and 1 per cent:				
4 Delaware	108	4,012	2.6	18.3
5 New York	730	29,217	2.5	8.5
6 California	597	25,010	2.3	5.6
7 New Jersey	340	16,197	2.1	8.5
8 Oklahoma	224	11,213	2.0	6.9
9 Pennsylvania	443	21,344	2.0	7.5
10 West Virginia	76	3,823	1.9	5.0
11 Ohio	323	17,146	1.8	8.1
12 Michigan	159	10,887	1.5	9.2
13 Arizona	49	3,474	1.4	3.0
14 New Mexico	41	3,641	1.1	2.0
15 Missouri	100	9,789	1.0	9.0
16 Nevada	28	2,634	1.0	5.0

(continued)

TABLE 19 - Continued

State	Total No. of Negroes in Guard (1964)	Total Unit Strength (1964)	% of Negroes in Guard	% of Negroes in State Population (1960)
States with between 1 and .1 per cent:				
17 Colorado	27	3,585	.8	2.0
18 Kentucky	41	5,362	.8	8.0
19 Texas	148	17,719	.8	14.2
20 Washington	54	6,801	.8	1.7
21 Indiana	74	10,583	.7	5.8
22 North Carolina	81	11,553	.7	24.9
23 Tennessee	100	12,730	.6	18.3
24 Kansas	37	7,524	.5	4.0
25 Massachusetts	90	16,233	.5	2.3
26 Rhode Island	18	3,459	.5	2.0
27 Connecticut	35	6,585	.4	4.2
28 Alaska	7	2,130	.3	2.5
29 Florida	23	7,935	.3	21.8
30 Oregon	14	6,661	.2	1.0
31 Wyoming	3	1,802	.15	1.0
32 Minnesota	16	11,675	.1	.6
States with between .1 and .01 per cent:				
33 Montana	3	3,074	.09	.2
34 Hawaii	5	4,970	.09	8.0
35 Utah	5	5,394	.09	3.0

TABLE 19 - Continued

	State	Total No. of Negroes in Guard (1964)	Total Unit Strength (1964)	% of Negroes in Guard	% of Negroes in State Population (1960)
36	Vermont	3	3,454	.08	1.0
37	Louisiana	5	7,729	.07	30.9
38	Wisconsin	8	10,387	.07	1.9
39	Iowa	5	9,387	.06	.9
40	South Carolina	6	9,915	.06	34.5
41	Virginia	5	7,694	.06	20.9
42	Maine	2	3,405	.05	3.0
43	Georgia	4	10,429	.04	31.1
44	Arkansas	4	8,836	.04	22.3
45	New Hampshire	1	2,690	.04	1.0
46	Nebraska	1	4,241	.02	2.0
47	Alabama	2	16,700	.01	30.0
48	Mississippi	2	11,431	.01	42.0
	States with 0 participation:				
49	Idaho	0	3,705	0	.5
50	North Dakota	0	3,382	0	.5
51	South Dakota	0	4,345	0	.5

Source: Computed from Table 18.

TABLE 20

Ranking of States by Ratio of Percentage of Negroes in
Guard to Percentage in Population

State	Index Illustrating Negro Guard Participation in Relation to State Negro Population	Groupment
New Mexico	.55	
District of Columbia	.54	
Illinois	.54	
Arizona	.47	
Washington	.47	
Maryland	.46	
Montana	.40	
Colorado	.40	
West Virginia	.38	
California	.30	
Utah	.30	Group I: 12 of first
New Hampshire	.30	18 states are urban
Oklahoma	.29	and industrial.
New York	.29	
Pennsylvania	.27	
Ohio	.22	
Rhode Island	.21	
New Jersey	.25	
Massachusetts	.21	
Nevada	.20	
Oregon	.20	
Minnesota	.16	
Maine	.16	
Michigan	.16	
Wyoming	.15	
Delaware	.14	
Alaska	.12	
Kansas	.12	Group II: 13 of
Hawaii	.11	middle 16 states
Missouri	.11	are rural, North-
Kentucky	.10	ern or Western.
Indiana	.10	
Nebraska	.10	
Connecticut	.09	
Vermont	.08	

TABLE 20 - Continued

State	Index Illustrating Negro Guard Participation in Relation to State Negro Population	Groupment
Texas	.06	
Wisconsin	.06	
Iowa	.06	
North Carolina	.03	
Tennessee	.03	
Florida	.01	Group III: 11 out of
Virginia	.003	the last 14 states
South Carolina	.002	are rural and
Louisiana	.002	Southern.
Arkansas	.002	
Georgia	.001	
Alabama	.0003	
Mississippi	.0002	

Note: Idaho and North and South Dakota have no Negroes in the Guard.

Source: Computed from Table 19.

TABLE 21

Change in Number of Negroes Serving in the National Guard (Army/Air Guard) in Eleven Southern States, 1964-65

State	1964		1965		% of Negroes in State Population (1960)	Total Number of Men in State Guard (1964)
	Army	Air	Army	Air		
Alabama	0	2	5	1	30.0	16,800
Arkansas	3	1	7	1	22.3	8,845
Florida	21	2	44	2	21.8	7,935
Georgia	2	2	1	2	31.1	10,429
Louisiana	3	2	1	2	30.9	7,629
Mississippi	1	1	24	6	42.0	11,431
North Carolina	80	1	106	1	24.9	11,553
South Carolina	1	5	5	5	34.5	9,915
Tennessee	94	6	118	13	18.3	12,720
Texas	146	2	178	5	14.15	17,719
Virginia	5	0	8	4	20.9	7,694
TOTALS	356	24	497	42		122,670

Net Increase: +141/+18
% Increase: 40%/75%

Source: Unpublished information obtained from Civil Rights Office, Department of Defense.

state Guard have the prerogative to recruit and reject or accept members assigned to their units, thus allowing majority
local prejudices to prevail over the minority. [67] Furthermore,
the Guard mainly drills in home-town armories, subsequently,
helping to control its exclusiveness through geographic im-
mobility. [68] Thus the Guard--predominantly nationally supported with quasi-federal obligations--has its internal policies
and membership largely controlled by local influences.

Until recently, the Negroes' inability to bring political
pressure on these local influences has been the chief reason
for their low representation in the Guard. The Voting Rights
Law of 1965 should help to remedy this situation, as more
Negroes register, vote, and demand equal opportunities in
communities.

Why does not the government use Title VI of the 1964
Civil Rights Act to threaten to reduce federal aid to states not
admitting Negroes to the Guard? Title VI reads: "No person
shall, on the grounds of race, color, or national origin, be
excluded from participation in, be denied benefit of, or be
subject to discrimination under any program or activity re-
ceiving Federal financial assistance. "[69]

The idea is appealing, but difficult to undertake. Some
states that have no Negro representation in Guard units have
virtually no Negroes in their states, Idaho, for example, lists
none in Guard activities and 1 per cent in the state population.
Some Guard units are all-Negro because there are only Negroes in the surrounding area. Harlem's 369th Regiment is
all-black because Negroes live there, have traditionally
formed this historic regiment, and take pride in keeping it
that way. Thus, the pattern of Negro distribution within our
nation deeply influences the membership of an organization
that recruits from local surroundings.

But what about states where there are many Negroes and
few in the Guard, as in the South? Here, Negroes often have
little interest in joining Guard activities. In Georgia, for example, where Martin Luther King and Julian Bond, two noted
Negro advocates of nonviolence, are leaders of the colored
community, it is almost a contradiction of their own philosophy
to ask for military rights in the Guard. [70] The political goals
of Negroes in many areas place little emphasis on military
demands.

White Southern leaders are making very real efforts to attract Negroes into the Guard, but partly because of the long history of Negro exclusion, the views of the present Negro leadership, and the more attractive uniformed service in the regular military, the response to their initial recruiting efforts has been small.   Mark S. Watson, a writer for the Baltimore Sun who has spent considerable time researching this problem, has concluded:

> The National Guard Bureau exhibited reports
> from the adjutants general of South Carolina,
> Georgia, and Arkansas which indicate in those
> states not merely an acceptance of orders from
> above but a genuine effort to bring qualified Ne-
> groes into Guard duty. . . . In Arkansas the openings
> continue for officer personnel for navigator as-
> signment in the Air Guard. In South Carolina it
> was stated that all Negro applicants who passed
> the tests had been offered duty. . . . In Georgia
> there was assurance that applicants, notably for
> the hospital unit, had proven acceptable and had
> been invited to enlist. . . . In Texas, the start had
> been poor, but present growth is improving
> slightly. In South Carolina, it was added, direct
> recruiting efforts have been conducted with the
> National Association for the Advancement of
> Colored People, with the Negroes in schools and
> in Federal, State, and city bureaus, and in
> homes. . . . The results in many cases are indeed
> "token. "[71]

If Negroes made strong local demands to join Guard units, Title VI could easily be applied by the Defense Department to remove barriers to their participation. In fact, individual state units are looking for interested Negroes. But a real difference exists between what the Negroes say they want at the national level--greater participation in federally assisted programs--and the number that actually apply at the community level to join the Guard. Negro leaders' national ideals ought to follow local demands, or local demands ought to be mobilized to better live up to national ideals.

Even though political power of Negroes will be the prime source of any improvement in their Guard participation, the

Pentagon can be criticized for its unwillingness to talk publicly about the issue. When Assistant Secretary of Defense
Carlisle P. Runge was asked about cutting funds for Guards
that openly excluded Negroes, he replied:

> To take action which might for all practical
> purposes eliminate a substantial proportion
> of the major reserve capability of our Guard
> and our forces is a matter which counsels
> the utmost caution in these perilous times. [72]

Instead of counseling caution, Runge could have made a clearer
directive that the Defense Department wants to see Negroes in
the National Guard. He could have taken the opportunity to
welcome their participation rather than offer an excuse for in-
action. A check of officers in the National Guard Bureau met
this same unwillingness to talk openly about what they consider
the touchy subject of civil rights. [73] Frankness, openness,
direct encouragement, and continual publicity would gain much
more than the policy of desperate quietude that both civilian
and military Defense administrators seem bound to follow.

THE KENNEDY-JOHNSON RE-EVALUATION

The 1960 Presidential race was won by a hair's-breadth.
John Kennedy received 49. 7 per cent of the popular vote;
Richard Nixon won 49. 6 per cent. [74] Brzezinski and Huntington's Political Power: USA/USSR related how decisive the
colored vote was to Kennedy's victory:

> Kennedy's success depended largely upon his
> carrying the large northern industrial states of
> New York, Pennsylvania, Ohio, Michigan, and
> Illinois. In all these states the Negro vote was
> crucial: Negroes made up 14 per cent of the
> population in New York City, 26 per cent in
> Philadelphia, 29 per cent in Detroit. Kennedy
> consequently made a strong appeal on civil rights:
> he denounced the failure of President Eisenhower
> to eliminate discrimination in federal housing
> "by a stroke of his pen"; he asked Senator Clark
> and Representative Celler to draw up legislation
> embodying the Democratic civil-rights plans;
> and at the climax of the campaign in the last

week of October, Kennedy telephoned the wife
of Martin Luther King offering his help and
sympathy on behalf of her husband, who had been
locked up in a Georgia prison for participating
in a civil-rights demonstration. This timely
gesture cemented the Negroes to the Kennedy
cause. In 1956, in the large cities of the north,
Stevenson had received about 65 per cent of the
Negro vote; Kennedy got about 75 per cent. In
an election as close as that of 1960, every vote
is decisive, and the strategically located Negro
vote was certainly no less so than any other. [75]

But Kennedy, after being elected, was not quick to move
on civil-rights issues, as Political Power explained:

The Kennedy Administration's own sense of needs
of the nation combined with the differences between its policy and electoral constituencies thus
led to a go-easy policy on civil rights during its
first two years. The two chief needs of the Negroes, in the Administration's view, were to
improve his economic position throughout the
country and to increase Negro voting in the South.
The best way to accomplish the first goal, the
Administration held, was to stimulate the economy
generally and to enact the Administration's social
welfare proposals. Hence, influence should be
directed to getting these measures through Congress rather than proposing major new civil-
rights legislation. "Suppose the President were
to send up a dramatic message on civil rights, "
as one Presidential assistant put it, "and alienate
enough Southerners to kill his economic program
in Congress. Would the Negro be better off? I'd
think he'd be worse off. "[76]

It took the quickened pace of violence at Oxford, Mississippi, and Birmingham, Alabama, in late 1962 and early 1963
to accelerate Kennedy's actions on civil-rights problems. As
the crisis heightened, Kennedy became more concerned over
civil rights.

The President took up Negro problems on many fronts.
One was the Negroes' relationship to the Defense Department.

The reappraisal begun under Kennedy and continued by President Johnson led to three achievements: 1) collection and evaluation of quantitative data on the Negroes in the armed forces; 2) the establishment of an office devoted to Negro concerns at the Department of Defense level in the Pentagon; 3) certain administrative actions to strengthen the Negro position in the military.

For the first time since Project CLEAR, the Administration collected hard data on Negro servicemen and attempted to give meaning to it. The undertaking was first urged in a 246-page report by the Presidential Commission on Civil Rights issued on October 14, 1961. [77] On June 22, 1962, Kennedy established a Committee on Equal Opportunity in the armed forces, and urged the committee to study two questions:

1. What measures should be taken to improve the effectiveness of current policies and procedures in the Armed Forces with regard to equality of treatment and opportunity for persons in the Armed Forces?
2. What measures should be employed to improve equality of opportunity for members of the Armed Forces and their dependents in the civilian community, particularly with respect to housing, education, transportation, recreational facilities, community events, programs and activities?[78]

"He was especially concerned that they should have as accurate data as possible," said Gerhard A. Gesell, a Washington lawyer and chairman of the committee. [79] Six others assisted him: Nathaniel S. Colley, Abe Fortas, Louis J. Hector, Benjamin Muse, John H. Sengstacke, and Whitney M. Young, Jr. [80] The committee interviewed individuals, heard complaints from whites and Negroes, and called upon Executive departments for data. It issued a report in two stages: Discrimination on base and off base was discussed in the June 13, 1963, part, and military personnel stationed overseas and in the National Guard in the November 30, 1964, part.

The report was invaluable, for it presented for the first time since the Truman Administration a quantitative picture of the Negro-military relationship. And only on the basis of pertinent statistics can administrative action be carefully undertaken.

The Gesell Report clearly presented the problems of imbalanced distribution of Negroes in the services, community relations, and the National Guard. But, without offering substantial factual proof, it ineffectually argued that there was on-base and overseas discrimination of Negro personnel. The case seemed to be contrived to please Negroes rather than to convince any military leaders. If the Gesell Report had focused on the three critical problems mentioned below and avoided this unconvincing argument, it might have won more armed-services decision-makers over to its viewpoint. [81]

The Gesell Report also suffered from an inadequate realization of the pressures for imbalanced distribution of Negroes, problems in community relations, and tensions in the National Guard. The social structure of the Negro community, automation in the military establishment, and the importance of the local power structure are three important influences on Negro military relations today, but they received little attention. [82] Yet understanding these is important to framing any reforms.

A third weakness lay in the fact that the report's solutions rested on the local base commander and urged the post to work out its own problems. But local military men are ill-suited for improving conditions in these amorphous areas. They lack training in racial matters. They need specific direction and supporting authority from above. If any improvements are to be made in local conditions, positive and negative threats must come from a higher level. Thus, the Pentagon, rather than base commanders, is required to improve the situation. [83]

Finally, the committee failed to see its recommendations through. It did not oversee administrative efforts necessary to remedy the problems. It made no provisions for continuing the review beyond the date of the last report, November 30, 1964. Continued systematic collection of data and continued independent thinking about these troublesome areas are essential, but now must await formation of a new presidential committee.

But the Gesell Committee was not the only innovation of the Kennedy-Johnson era. An office devoted to the Negro's concerns was established at the Department of Defense. After the first part of the Gesell Report was issued on June 13, 1963, President Kennedy ordered Secretary of Defense

Robert S. McNamara to give "prompt attention" to the Negroes' problems. His letter appears on the following page.

As a direct result of the Gesell Committee's findings,
the office of Deputy Assistant Secretary for Civil Rights and
Industrial Relations was created. (See Table 22, the current
organizational chart.) There have been other high-level racial
advisers. Emmett Scott was appointed an aide to Newton
Baker in World War I, and Lester Granger assisted James
Forrestal in World War II. But they served on a temporary,
ad hoc basis and left after the war ended. McNamara, however, succeeded in finding a permanent spot for the Negro
problem within the organization by establishing this Department of Defense high-level office. [84]

Alfred B. Fitt, former Army manpower chief, was the
first appointee, taking office on July 30, 1963. Within a year,
he was replaced by his aide, Steven Shulman. Within another
year, Jack Moskowitz took the post when Shulman left for a
position with the Air Force. [85] The background of these three
individuals was much the same: Caucasian, legally trained,
politically appointed, no training or enduring convictions in
racial affairs. They were novices who saw the office as a
steppingstone to a higher position rather than as a career objective in itself.

What the office requires is an able Negro having a long-
term dedication, prior knowledge, and sensitivity in racial
matters; a man who can win the Secretary of Defense to his
viewpoint, and not surrender to the Secretary of Defense; a man
who understands the workings of the military institution and
who can effectively use the powers of his office to achieve solutions in the amorphous areas.

Civil rights is not suited to the "whiz kid" breed of Pentagon administrator. Ideally, the appointee should possess
the authority and organizational talents of a Robert Weaver and
the determination and intellectual persuasiveness of a Thur-
good Marshall. Few men like that are available, but for such
a man the post offers a potential that has so far been unrealized.

One danger of appointing a Negro to this post is that he
could turn out to be a "company man." Instead of being a
spokesman for his race, he could become a mere "yes" man
for the Defense Secretary, thereby cutting the Secretary off

THE WHITE HOUSE
WASHINGTON

June 21, 1963

Dear Mr. Secretary:

Because of my concern that there be full equality of treatment
and opportunity for all military personnel, regardless of race
or color, I appointed a Committee to study the matter in June
of 1962. An initial report of my Committee on Equal Opportunity in the Armed Forces is transmitted with this letter for
your personal attention and action.

We have come a long way in the 15 years since President Truman ordered the desegregation of the Armed Forces. The
military services lead almost every other segment of our society in establishing equality of opportunity for all Americans.
Yet a great deal remains to be done.

As the report emphasizes, a serious morale problem is
created for Negro military personnel when various forms of
segregation and discrimination exist in communities neighboring military bases. Discriminatory practices are morally
wrong wherever they occur -- they are especially inequitable
and iniquitous when they inconvenience and embarrass those
serving in the Armed Services and their families. Responsible
citizens of all races in these communities should work together
to open up public accommodations and housing for Negro military personnel and their dependents. This effort is required
by the interests of our national defense, national policy and
basic considerations of human decency.

It is encouraging to note that the continuing effort over the last
fifteen years to provide equality of treatment and opportunity
for all military personnel on base is obviously having far-
reaching and satisfactory results. The remaining problems
outlined by the Committee pertaining to on-base conditions, of
course, must be remedied. All policies, procedures and conditions under which men and women serve must be free of
considerations of race or color.

The Committee's recommendations regarding both off-base and on-base conditions merit your prompt attention and certainly are in the spirit that I believe should characterize our approach to this matter. I would hope your review and report on the recommendations could be completed within 30 days.

I realize that I am asking the military community to take a leadership role, but I believe that this is proper. The Armed Services will, I am confident, be equal to the task. In this area, as in so many others, the U.S. Infantry motto "Follow Me" is an appropriate guide for action.

Sincerely

s/ John F. Kennedy

Honorable Robert S. McNamara
Secretary of Defense

Source: On file in Civil Rights Office, Department of Defense.

TABLE 22

Organizational Chart of the Office of Civil Rights and Industrial Relations,
Department of Defense

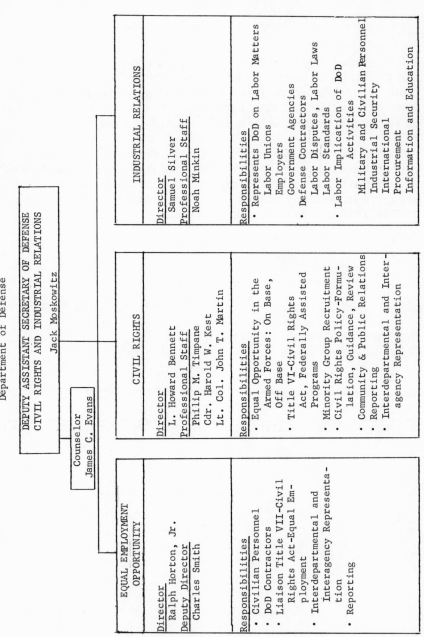

DEPUTY ASSISTANT SECRETARY OF DEFENSE
CIVIL RIGHTS AND INDUSTRIAL RELATIONS
Jack Moskowitz

Counselor
James C. Evans

EQUAL EMPLOYMENT OPPORTUNITY

Director
Ralph Horton, Jr.
Deputy Director
Charles Smith

Responsibilities
- Civilian Personnel
- DoD Contractors
- Liaison Title VII-Civil Rights Act-Equal Employment
- Interdepartmental and Interagency Representation
- Reporting

CIVIL RIGHTS

Director
L. Howard Bennett
Professional Staff
Philip M. Timpane
Cdr. Harold W. Kest
Lt. Col. John T. Martin

Responsibilities
- Equal Opportunity in the Armed Forces: On Base, Off Base
- Title VI-Civil Rights Act, Federally Assisted Programs
- Minority Group Recruitment
- Civil Rights Policy-Formulation, Guidance, Review
- Community & Public Relations
- Reporting
- Interdepartmental and Interagency Representation

INDUSTRIAL RELATIONS

Director
Samuel Silver
Professional Staff
Noah Minkin

Responsibilities
- Represents DoD on Labor Matters
  Labor Unions
  Employers
  Government Agencies
- Defense Contractors
  Labor Disputes, Labor Laws
  Labor Standards
- Labor Implication of DoD Activities
  Military and Civilian Personnel
  Industrial Security
  International
  Procurement
  Information and Education

114

from Negro thinking.   This was the situation in World War I, when Emmett Scott and Robert Moton had the ear of Secretary of War Newton Baker, to the loss of any dissenting colored voices.

How much could a dedicated Negro do in this office?   He would be one of twenty-eight Assistant Deputy Secretaries, each of whom has to go through one of eleven Deputy Secretaries to reach the ear of McNamara, who is currently occupied with Vietnam, with little time for civil-rights problems.

But because there are so few Negroes at the Department of Defense level (the first Negro, James Davenport, was appointed a Deputy Secretary of Defense in January),[86] a Negro in the post would increase the Negroes' high-level representation in the Pentagon and give them a good way to speak out and act on what really concerns them most.

Finally, viewing the third attribute of the Kennedy-Johnson re-evaluation of Negro-military relations, the following administrative actions were taken to strengthen the Negro position in the military:

1.   Integration of the Reserves was completed.   Although the Reserves had followed the pattern of armed-forces integration since 1948, six small all-colored units were still in existence in 1961.   (See Table 23.)   These were ordered integrated on April 3, 1962, by Roswell Gilpatrick, Deputy Secretary of Defense for Manpower.[87] On June 26, 1963, the Pentagon announced: "Such all-Negro units in the Reserves as were found to be in existence for whatever reason, have been integrated."[88]

2.   Token integration was achieved in the National Guard. At the time of Kennedy's election, several Southern states had legal statutes barring Negro participation.   By December 30, 1964, Major General Winston P. Wilson, head of the National Guard Bureau, could announce that: "token integration had been achieved in all National Guard units" and that "a steady growth was expected."[89]

3.   Verbal and administrative reforms reflected the services' commitment to integration:[90]

TABLE 23

Negro Participation in Ready Reserves, 1962

	Army	Navy	Air Force	Marine Corps
Total Number of Men	839,951	437,888	171,778	162,345
Total Negroes	40,439	13,972	7,588	17,797
Percentage of Negroes	4.8	3.2	4.4	4.8
Number of Units	4,090	3,048	902	229
Number of Negro Units	6	0	0	0

Source: Unpublished information obtained from Civil Rights Office, Department of Defense.

a. The Department of the Army established an Equal Rights Branch in the Office of the Deputy Chief of Staff for Personnel, and on July 2, 1964, issued guidance documents for military commanders--Army Regulation No. 600-21, "Equal Opportunity and Treatment of Military Personnel."

b. The Navy Department Created an ad hoc committee in the Bureau of Personnel that addressed itself to the problems of Negroes. The Department further issued Instruction No. 5350.6 on "Equal Opportunity and Treatment of Military Personnel."

c. The Department of the Air Force established an Air Force Committee on Equal Opportunity, April 19, 1963, and on August 19, 1964, issued Regulation No. 35-78, "Equal Opportunity and Treatment of Military Personnel."

d. At the Department of Defense level, Defense Secretary Robert S. McNamara issued a memo on July 26, 1963, that emphasized his commitment: "Every military commander has the responsibility to oppose discriminatory practices affecting his own men and their dependents and to foster equal opportunity, not only in his own areas under his command but also in nearby communities where men live or gather in off-duty hours."[91] Many memos have come from this office:[92] One requested commanders to cooperate with reputable voluntary groups of private citizens to seek open occupancy and adequate housing for their personnel; another ordered commanders not to participate in educational offerings at segregated schools; a third prevented units from participating in segregated functions.

But despite the stream of orders and administrative reforms, there have been few instances of the military forcing the private sector to integrate: the integration of a few trailer parks at Keesler Air Base in Mississippi, McGuire Air Base in New Jersey, and Monmouth Air Base in Arizona; an accelerated school-desegregation plan at Huntsville, Alabama, and Corpus Christi, Texas; and the integration of some homes near Fort Benning in Georgia and Craig Air Base in Alabama.[93] The Defense Department, despite all its administrative memos, has had little influence outside the post gate.

CHAPTER THE FUTURE AND
SIGNIFICANCE OF NEGRO-
MILITARY RELATIONSHIPS

THE EFFECT OF SOCIOLOGICAL
PROBLEMS AND CHANGES

The armed services will never return to the policy of
segregation of World War II, for this would never be permitted by the groups most concerned--the Negroes, the politicians,
and the defense organization. Yet this does not portend a
rising line of progress for colored men in the service. The
forces of exclusion and inclusion still operate in many direc-
tions--pushing the Negro into a lesser role and at the same
time prodding him toward equal status with whites. The next
twenty-five years will find a mixture of forces shaping the Negro's role in the military:

Negro Political Influence on the Military

If the Democratic consensus grows, Negro political influence on the military will decline. The Negroes are the
group most deeply committed to the Democratic Party. Three-
fourths of them voted for President Kennedy, and 85 per cent
for President Johnson. Historically, the Negroes have been
most influential in party politics when their votes have been
most sought after. When they were the pivotal swing group in
a national election, they have been the group most generously
rewarded by the President. Particularly in the services, Negroes have achieved more of their demands when the Demo-
crats won marginal victories.

If Johnson, however, realizes his ambition to establish
a broad base of support, a consensus--including right as well
as left, conservative and liberal, the Russells and the
Humphreys--the Negro would not be needed to win elections
and his demands, say in military privileges, would receive
considerably less attention from the sources of power and

reform.   The fringe groups, the less committed ones, would
reap greater rewards in order to be won over to the Democratic camp.   The most loyal followers, like the Negroes,
whose votes are taken for granted, would receive a smaller
share of the political spoils.   Logically, being a more de-
tached, independent swing group would be a wiser role in
coming elections for Negroes if they want to improve their
bargaining position in military issues.

Social Unrest and Negro-Military Relationships

If Negro middle-class frustration intensifies or is di-
verted to other areas, bargaining issues with the Defense Department will be less specified.   The nation continues to be
shaken by racial unrest.   Murders of civil-rights workers in
the South, de facto school segregation in the North, high unemployment among unskilled Negroes, low Negro voting reg-
istration, racially biased jury trials cause deep resentments,
often expressed by militant colored protest groups financed,
organized, and led by middle-class Negroes.   But their own
broad, idealistic demands, understandably stimulated by frustrations, can most weaken their political effectiveness.   For
if they use the military as an ideological whipping post on which
to vent their feelings of frustration, they will give little practical consideration to what the actual problems are and will
inaccurately direct the political forces for achieving reforms.
This frustration was reflected in Julian Bond's quotation from
a SNCC statement on Vietnam on March 4, 1966, at
Harvard:

> "We take note of the fact that 60% of the draftees
> from this country are Negroes called on to stifle
> the liberation of Vietnam...We are in sympathy
> with and support the men in this country who are
> unwilling to respond to a military draft which
> would compel them to contribute their lives in
> Vietnam in the name of freedom we find so false
> in this country. "[1]

Bond's pacifist views do not encourage a positive relationship
between the Negro and the military and could magnify their differences.

Or if Negro militants ignore military issues while turning
to fields like housing, voting, and schools, they will leave

unsolved the remaining issues of race relations in the armed
forces. If Negroes expect to make future gains, their middle-
class members, the major source of future reforms, must
understand the involved military issues, sharpen their demands, and apply pressure to achieve them. However, this
is made more difficult by the increased complexity of Negro-
military issues and the decreasing attention on these problems
by Negro groups.

Need for More Education and Training

If increased military automation, slow changes in Negro
class structure, and high competition for Negro middle-class
professionals continue, imbalanced distribution of Negroes in
uniform will increase. The Defense Department will continue
to be reshaped by greater needs for expertise. Since World
War II, the technician has been replacing the unskilled soldier.
A good indicator of the new skills required by the modern
infantryman is the 1st Air Cavalry Division, operating successfully in South Vietnam. Its 450 helicopters used to trans-
port men quickly in and out of battle zones require numbers of
pilots, maintenance men, and supply administrators that were
absent from the standard combat unit before Vietnam. Possible
future warfare will require increased mobility, higher fire-
power, more complex communications, so that greater specialized, scientific, and professional knowledge will be demanded in servicemen, from privates to generals.

Because many Negroes possess insufficient skills to cope
with rising automation, Negro unemployment is 8 per cent
(13 per cent for Negro teen-agers), compared with 4 per cent
for the nation as a whole. The immediate future offers little
hope of reshaping the Negro class structure to meet the growing demands for expertise in the military and elsewhere. The
armed services will find it more difficult to hold onto the
skilled Negroes they already have, due to competition from
business. Furthermore, sudden peace and a steep decline in
military strength would encourage a keen competition for
senior NCO and officer ranks in which whites would have the
advantage of greater skills. Subsequently, there may develop
an even larger divergence between white professional leadership and black semiskilled subordinates. The near future offers at best a status quo with plenty of opportunities for a more
uneven allocation of Negroes in the defense organization.

Inequality in Civilian Life

Continued organizational commitment to integration exists in the regular defense establishment, but continued shared local and state powers exacerbate inequality in the National Guard and nearby off-post. Between 1948 and 1953, military goals coincided with Negro demands. Improved efficiency in human organization--the armed forces' objective-- became equated with equality of opportunity--the Negroes' ideal. The two ends have since become solidly welded.

Nonetheless, local forces outside the scope of direct military authority will continue to affect the National Guard and off-post living. Though the armed forces have considerable powers to remedy these situations, the Negro community currently expresses little desire for political pressure to be applied to the military to obtain reforms. However, local Negro groups can achieve changes on the state and community levels in a slower, piecemeal fashion. In fact, the best stimulus for military reforms in the coming years will probably be not Pentagon direction but local colored people exercising their new federal privileges in suffrage, education, public accommodations, and employment.

Improved Ability--but Reduced Priorities-- for Military Reform

While the Negro community suffers a growing gap between its ideals and its abilities to achieve them, the armed services have moved in the opposite direction: Their powers to effect improvement in the racial situation have improved, but they have reduced interest in making racial reforms.

Today, there is greater unified civilian authority running the Defense Department. Under McNamara, civilian defense managers sharply tightened control over military decisions and increased unity in defense planning.[2] Bombing decisions for Vietnam were made in McNamara's office, not at General Westmoreland's field command.[3] This is the reverse of the situation in the immediate postwar period, when the military chiefs in each department--Bradley, Eisenhower, MacArthur, LeMay, Twining, Nimitz--exerted the greatest influence over Defense decisions. For race relations, this greater centralization has increased the authority for reform-- the office of Assistant Secretary of Defense for Civil Rights and Industrial Relations, the ability to collect and publish regularly racial statistics, the capability of creating positive incentives through military orders, monetary inducements or institutional reorganization. But since 1963, there has been a reduction in the organizational priorities to make these powers work. The demands of an enlarging Vietnam war and the Negroes' reduced capability to bargain with the military has made the centralized authority dormant, possessing real capability but lacking effective leadership. There is today a better structure for effecting racial reforms, but the critical question is: Will it be used?

Benefits from Military Integration

Continued positive returns are realized by the military, white, and nonwhite communities from the present integrated relationship: Hardly a day passes without a news picture showing white and colored soldiers arm in arm on a Vietnam battlefield. Clearly, life is more equal for the Negro in the armed forces than in civilian communities. Here he can forget the problems of race and receive good pay, patriotic fulfillment, and society's recognition. Indeed, he must be won over by these rewards, for colored voluntary enlistment is currently 13 per cent, compared with the colored community's 11.9 per cent of the national population. Moreover, the Negroes have a 49.3-per-cent re-enlistment rate, compared with 18.5 per cent for whites. Jack Moskowitz, Deputy Assistant Secretary of Defense for Civil Rights and Industrial Relations, put it succinctly: "That uniform gives prestige and status to a guy who's been 100 years on the back burner."[4]

However, the military is more than just a materially better place for Negroes. The armed forces is the colored man's haven from worldly oppression, a medieval cloister in a modern society. When he answers its call and serves it with devotion, the military gains the men it needs to fight wars, occupy territory, run ships and planes, and file orders. In turn, the Negro is sheltered from worldly prejudices. If he adopts the ideals of the profession, follows its discipline, isolates himself from the political world, and permits the acquired expertise to shape his character, the military will make his soul an equal one, and so the Negro in uniform must feel the rewards that only religious faith bestows on the devout.

The services' authority frees the Negro from choices that have humiliated him and even holds out a hope that if things are better here, they may someday be better in civilian life.

The average American white shares in these spiritual benefits. His conscience rejoices that the military--which he pays taxes to maintain--is treating the Negro fairly. But this integration remains distant from his life. Perhaps he may serve a couple of years in the Army, but other than that, he has no contact with the services or their integration. His attitude toward the distant military differs sharply from his attitude toward segregation in his neighborhood. The far-off military achievement can quiet the pangs of conscience caused by his behavior in his community.

Thus, integration of the services offers continuing rewards to three groups--for the Negro, an institutional haven; for the military, troops to fill its ranks; and for the American white, a salve for his conscience.

POLITICAL CONDITIONS NECESSARY TO DEVELOP HUMAN EQUALITY

The American ideals have traditionally stressed human equality. Yet the American democracy has produced great inequities in wealth, races, and social classes--particularly in regard to Negroes. This study viewed one area where the Negro has come closer to realizing the American ideals than anywhere else in our society. What he found in the military was not perfect equality with the white but a clear improvement over his civilian life. If there is significance to the Negro's participation in the military, it is that it demonstrates conditions that make his life better. What are the political conditions that develop human equality in the armed forces and are essential for minority opportunity in civilian life?

Importance of a Reform-Minded, Minority Middle Class

Under the American political system, a minority group is capable of asserting itself when a group within it desires personal equality with other Americans and has the abilities to make the desired reforms possible. The lower class within a minority is generally too poor, too illiterate, and too lacking in public spirit to dedicate itself to such ventures. The upper classes often create their own social world and divorce themselves from the rest of their race as well as the general society.   The middle class of the minority have education, convictions, and some funds, which the poor lack, but they do not possess the sums and/or distinctions to fashion their own worlds, as can the upper-class members.   The middle class is often the group with the greatest discrepancy between personal goals and achievements, and is often first to voice its frustrations at not fully sharing in the rewards of the community.

Within a minority, the middle-class group is the very essence of that class's drive to obtain equality within the system.   Without its idealistic, reform-minded individuals, integration in the armed forces would have remained a barren hope.   One of the greatest obstacles to Negro advancement in American history has been the small size of this critical class, the enormous preponderance of the illiterate, unskilled lower class, and the alienation of upper-class Negroes from white middle-class America, as in the case of W. E. B. DuBois, and from the aspirations of their own race, as in the case of Booker T. Washington. [5] The Negro political group has suffered from a complete lack of leadership, organization, and convictions, within a democratic society that strongly demands these qualities in any participating political faction.

However, the Negro middle class has its own limitation. Too much idealism lessens the effectiveness of protest; it can misread what is happening and misdirect the group's efforts to achieve reforms.   The Negro protest over the military in the 1950's failed to see the new problems and adjust demands accordingly.   Thus, the reformers' strength, their spirited protest, can be the very source of their blindness and consequent political weakness.

Protection of a Strong, Authoritarian, Hierarchical Organization

The irony is that the least democratic organization, the armed forces, has introduced equality most rapidly in America.

Since World War II, America has witnessed the most rapid achievement of human equality in an organizational

structure that regiments life and permits small individual
diversity. After the goals of the organization were established by outside forces, beginning in 1948, the armed forces
employed its capabilities of specialization, high mobility,
professional isolation, and entrance requirements to give
equality to Negroes.

But the armed forces had been just as efficient in World
War II in achieving a higher degree of Negro segregation in
military life than existed in civilian communities. Organizational structure is merely the means of achieving equality,
not the reason for it. The play of political forces around the
organization largely determines the values of a regimented
body.

The Necessity of Communications--Effective Use of Bargaining Power

In a democracy, the majority rules. How, then, does a
minority achieve its ends? One way is through political bargaining. Their talent at voicing their demands and utilizing
threats to sway the majority to their viewpoint can make the
difference between political strength (attaining what they want)
and political weakness (doing without). The Negroes' experience with the military in 1948 is a good example of a small
faction's influencing a large bureaucracy. The Negroes timed
their demands for integration to coincide with the 1948 draft
law and the 1948 election. They specified their goals publicly,
firmly committed themselves to their positions, and organized
a convincing threat of action--draft evasion and denial of political support in the coming election--if their demands were
not met. Furthermore, they found alliances with sympathetic
liberal groups--the ADA, Jews, labor, and churches. When
Truman issued the executive order, they dropped their threat
of draft evasion and supported his bid for the Presidency.

Such give-and-take is essential for minorities in the
American political system if they are to achieve their desires
at the national level. Failure of minorities to apply effective
pressures and "play politics" makes them impotent and costs
them their gains. The Southerners have long recognized this,
and have been effective in turning their minority into a potent
national force. Other minorities would do well to study their
example.

Interdependent Structural Needs
and Minority Demands

Humans who live together have common needs; the closer these desires are, the greater the common interest in working and living together. The positions of the military and the Negro have been closest when the two groups have shared strong mutually interdependent needs. Their needs have been totally different, but could be achieved only when both participated together. The armed forces is a large organization needing enormous manpower. The Negro community is a racial group desiring social recognition and economic benefits. The more intensely these needs have been felt by both bodies, the closer together they have moved. The less strongly these desires have been expressed by one or both factions, the more separated they have been.

For minorities in general, this means they can achieve higher equality when they express their demands as well as adapt themselves to the needs of society or groups within the society. It is a two-way street, for they must tell others what they want as well as lend an ear to what other people want from them. If needs are clearly expressed, mutually shared, and are of a continuing nature, the structure for a strong and enduring relationship will have been framed.

Parallel Minority-Class Structure with
Organizational Role Requirements

The greatest weakness of the Negro-military relationship now is that professional jobs in the armed forces cannot be filled by the predominance of lower-class semiskilled Negroes.

No skills in America today are for whites only, but the employment of Negroes in low-prestige jobs is encouraged by long tradition as well as lack of education. Some Negroes conjure up the image of a sleeping-car porter, entertainer, sports performer, or waiter simply because Negroes are often found in these roles. Dispersion of talents among other realms of human endeavors would break down society's stereotype of the Negro. Thus, wider employment diversification through improved education would serve a dual purpose: fill the social unit's demands at various levels of competence and prevent the categorizing of a group by occupation.

High Competition Between Political Groups
for Minority Support

The Negroes' position in the defense establishment has improved the most when they comprised the swing group in a political election. In 1866, the Republicans courted their support by establishing Negro military units. In 1948, Truman sought their favor by his executive order. In 1960, the Negroes' contribution to Kennedy's close victory brought a re-evaluation of their role in the services. But when political groups have not cared how the Negroes voted, their demands for equal opportunity in the armed forces have fallen upon deaf ears. During the era of World War I and World War II, the Negroes had small effect on the outcome of elections and, consequently, failed to get what they wanted from the armed forces. Under a good democratic system, politicians are responsive only to votes. If the Negroes do not strategically make their votes influential, they will gain few political goals.

High competition between political groups for minority support requires something of the system and something of the minority faction. The system must provide a close parity of party strength, ample rewards for the victorious, and political actors whose prime design is to pursue votes, not ideals. The minority must be capable of strategic voting-- in other words, placing themselves in an independent, swing-group position, waiting for the political combatants to raise the stakes for their votes, and then at the last moment casting them for the man who will be the winner and reward the group the most. This ideal situation requires considerable sophistication from both the political system and the minority. If the Negroes can maneuver this situation, they can achieve considerably more equality than before the situation of high competition occurred.

Summary

Human equality can be developed only under the right combination of political conditions. In the Negro-military experience can be found convenient tests by which an advanced democratic nation can determine what these conditions are.

Does the minority have a strong, vocal, community-minded middle class? Does an authoritarian, hierarchical

structure serve to protect their rights? Can the group com-
municate their interests and use bargaining strategies to
achieve their goals? Will there be a unity between the society's
and minority's goals? Does the social structure of the race
parallel the social structure of the general community? Is
there a high competition for the political resources of the
minority by politicians?

From the armed-forces experiences, it was observed
that the stronger the affirmative replies to these questions,
the stronger was the acceptance of the Negro in the armed
forces. The more negative responses received, the greater
his rejection.

The armed forces, while still not fully answering yes to
all questions, is perhaps the institution in American culture that
is closest to containing these political equality-producing components and, consequently, has so far achieved the highest
form of integration. A small Southern town has perhaps the
fewest of these attributes and thus the highest form of exclu-
sion--few vocal middle-class Negroes, a city government
shot through with local influences, a large, semi-illiterate,
poor colored population, a large divergence between the status-
quo ends of the white power structure and the economic-welfare
goals of lower-class Negroes, a wide difference between
majority- and minority-class structure, and virtually no need
for Negro votes to elect community leaders. Fortunately,
federal action is changing this pattern. But nevertheless, the
political variables that foster military inclusion of the Negro
offer a sharp contrast to Southern conditions that support his
exclusion.

APPLYING THE MILITARY EXPERIENCE
TO CIVILIAN LIFE

The South Post of Fort Myer houses servicemen and
their families who work at the Pentagon. The post is a typical
military base with mud-brown houses, troop barracks, a PX,
a chapel, a commissary, all laid out in neat geometric patterns. The soldiers in their khaki uniforms, from the military policemen at the gate to the privates on the drill field,
blend into the disciplined, symmetrical setting. Moving unnoticed in this ordered scene is an individual whose numbers
make up better than one-tenth of the post's population, the

Negro. It takes a special effort to realize that here white and
Negro families live next door to each other; their children
play together and without exception attend a post school; the
wives shop in the PX and pray in the same chapel pews; the
husbands find a common enjoyment at the officer's club as
well as on the bowling team. In social activities as well as
at work, racial identity is lost, for here all men wear the
same uniform, receive pay and privileges according to rank,
and work in common to achieve military goals. The worth of
the individual is judged by values other than race: How competent is he? What rank does he hold?

A mile down Route 95 toward Richmond, bounded by the
highway and the Army-Navy Country Club, is a Negro area in
the city of Arlington. As in most American cities, large or
small, Arlington's Negro citizens live in one area. Despite
the community's upper-middle-class income, educational level,
and moderate liberal orientation, this section has decaying
homes, the city's highest crime rate, an overcrowded, all colored
elementary and junior high school, homes where the father
works at unskilled labor, or where he is unemployed, or where
there is no father at all. Most worship in a colored Baptist
church and find their Saturday-night entertainment at a local
bar. There, a white visitor feels like an alien, and blacks
stare when a white enters their territory. Just across the
four-lane Route 95 is white man's land. Here there are three
newly built apartment houses. Near by there are suburban
homes, ranch-style, with neatly trimmed lawns. Here upper-
middle-income professional families live. Neighborhood
schools, churches, recreational areas, shopping centers are
frequented by whites. Trees along the road prevent them from
seeing those on the other side of the highway. Their nearest
association is the occasional cleaning woman who walks past
their homes in the early morning and late evening.

On the surface it seems the typical American community
has not progressed much since 1835, when Alexis de Tocqueville acutely observed:

> Whoever has inhabited the United States must
> have perceived that in those parts of the Union
> in which the Negroes are no longer slaves they
> have in no way drawn nearer to the whites. On
> the contrary, the prejudice of race appears to
> be stronger in the states that have abolished

> slavery than in those where it still exists; and
> nowhere is it so intolerant as in those states
> where servitude has never been known... they
> may bring an action at law, but they will find
> none but whites among their judges; and although
> they may legally serve as jurors, prejudice
> repels them from that office. The same schools
> do not receive the children of the black and of
> the European. In the theaters gold cannot pro-
> cure a seat for the servile race beside their
> former masters; in the hospitals they lie apart;
> and although they are allowed to invoke the same
> God as the whites, it must be at a different altar
> and in their own churches, with their own clergy. [6]

Several journalists have looked with considerable curi-
osity at the contrast between the lives of Negroes in civilian
communities like Arlington and in the military surroundings
like Fort Myer since integration occurred there, in 1953. In
print, they keep asking Are not Negroes better off in the
military than the civilian world? Perhaps. But cannot the
military experience be applied in the civilian world? What is
its significance for America?

Morton Puner, in the June, 1959, issue of Coronet magazine, summarized:

> Through integration, our mighty defense
> machinery, with all its potential for destruc-
> tion, is sowing the seeds of brotherly love
> and understanding among Americans. [7]

Lee Nichols, in Breakthrough on the Colored Front
(1954), concluded:

> How had the military acted as a spearhead toward
> nonsegregation throughout the United States?
>
> First, by power of example. By knocking
> down its racial barriers, the military had shown
> it could be done, that Negroes and whites...
> would work, live, and play together with little
> or no concern once they got used to the idea.

Secondly, there was not a way to bottle up
racial integration within the military post.   Men
leaving the service were taking back to civilian
life at least some of their new experience.   Part
might wear off among men returning to rigidly
segregated communities.

A third impact was in direct military contacts
with outside communities.   Integration was
spilling over incontrollably.   Churches, USO
clubs, cafes, taxi cabs, in the north and south,
here and there, began voluntarily to admit
Negroes on equal or near equal basis with white
servicemen. [8]

What has been the application of the military experience
to the civilian communities? Are the writers correct in their
estimations? Has the military sown "seeds of brotherly love"
as Puner suggests? Has it been an influence "knocking down
racial barriers" elsewhere as Nichols indicates? What impact has it had?

The framework developed by this writer for viewing the
dynamics of Negro-military relations was based upon the
special political conditions operating in military life.   These
have promoted the higher, though still not perfect, equality
between races found in uniform.   Furthermore, it was suggested that perhaps the political components of development
here could be a suitable test for analyzing governmental weak-
nesses elsewhere.   But to imply that the experience of the Negro-military relationship can be applied in civilian life to promote equality fails to take realistic account of the peculiar
forces at work here and found nowhere else.

But while application outside the post gate is restricted,
this does not mean within the military setting, in the realm
where inclusionary and exclusionary forces are still at work,
the Negro's position ought not or cannot be improved.
The men at the helm in the Pentagon have the authority to develop programs and to implement actions for the betterment
of the Negro in the armed forces.   These leaders have con-
structive options available to avoid much of the rough weather.
How they steer the rudder will have an impact on the effectiveness of the Vietnam operations, the attitudes of the Negro community, and, ultimately, the nation's well being.   Will they be
able to master their own ship's destiny?

NOTES

NOTES

NOTES TO CHAPTER 1

1. Essentially this concept follows Lasswell's definition of
politics as distribution of privileges by influence and the influential.
"Who should be where, when, and how" is utilizing this concept as
it relates to military organizational decision-making concerning
racial policies. For a further idea of Lasswellian thinking, refer
to: Harold D. Lasswell, Politics (New York: Whittlesey House,
1936), p. 1.

2. Chapter 2 considers Washington's exclusionary policies.

3. Chapter 4 and Chapter 5 discuss this issue.

4. Brown v. the Board of Education of Topeka, 347 U.S. 483
(1954).

5. Chapter 3 and Chapter 4 contain several tables which explain the important aspects of Negro and military class structure
and how they relate to each other.

6. This view of the military profession as "managers of violence"
is used in: Harold D. Lasswell, Politics, Who Gets What, Where,
When, and How (New York: Peter Smith, 1951), Chap. IV.

7. While many of Myrdal's statistics are now outdated, his
book was the father of all current sociological investigations, and
its basic conceptualization of the problem is still relevant: Gunnar
Myrdal, An American Dilemma (New York: Harper, 1944). For a
more recent investigation and interpretation of American Negroes,
see: Thomas F. Pettigrew, A Profile of the Negro American
(Princeton, N.J.: Van Nostrand, 1964); or Charles E. Silberman,
Crisis in Black and White (New York: Random House, 1963); or
Nathaniel Glazer and Daniel Patrick Moynihan, Beyond the Melting
Pot: The Negroes, Puerto Ricans, Jews, Italians, and Irish of
New York City (Cambridge, Mass.: M.I.T. Press, 1963).

8. For civil-military relations, see: Samuel P. Huntington, The Soldier and the State: The Theory and Politics of Civil-Military Relations (Cambridge, Mass.: Harvard, 1957) pp. 211-21.

9. James Q. Wilson, Negro Politics (Glencoe, Ill: Free Press, 1960), pp. 133-69; and Glazer and Moynihan, op. cit., pp. 67-87.

10. Huntington, op. cit., Chap. IV, VIII, and XI.

11. For discussion of historical restraints on Negroes in America, refer to: Kenneth M. Stampp, The Peculiar Institution (New York: Knopf, 1956); Leon F. Litwack, North of Slavery: The Negro in the Free States, 1790-1860 (Chicago: University of Chicago, 1961); and C. Vann Woodward, The Strange Career of Jim Crow (New York: Oxford University Press, 1957).

12. For a broad understanding of Negro history, refer to: John Hope Franklin, From Slavery to Freedom: A History of American Negroes (New York: Knopf, 1956).

13. Ibid.

14. Role in Vietnam is discussed in Chapter 4 and Chapter 5.

15. "Only One Color," Newsweek (December 6, 1965), pp. 42-43.

16. World War II role is considered in Chapter 3.

17. Ibid.

18. Ibid.

19. Jean Byers, "Study of the Negro in Military Service" (unpublished manuscript in Pentagon, U.S. Army Library, Washington, D.C.), June, 1947, p. 52.

NOTES TO CHAPTER 2

1. An excellent description of the colored individual's colonial status in America is found in Oscar Handlin, Race and Nationality in American Life (New York: Doubleday, 1957), particularly Chap. I. For founding fathers' attitudes toward Negroes, see Max Farrand, The Framing of the Constitution of the United States (New York: Yale, 1913).

2. Benjamin A. Quarles, The Negro in the American Revolution (Chapel Hill: University of North Carolina, 1961).

3. John Hope Franklin, From Slavery to Freedom: A History of American Negroes (New York: Knopf, 1956), pp. 130-40.

4. Ibid.

5. Quarles, op. cit.

6. Ibid.

7. Franklin, op. cit.

8. Ibid.

9. Refer to Kenneth M. Stampp, The Peculiar Institution (New York: Knopf, 1956); Leon F. Litwack, North of Slavery: The Negro in the Free States, 1790-1860 (Chicago: University of Chicago, 1961).

10. Rayford W. Logan, "The Negro in the Quasi War, 1798-1800," Negro History Bulletin, XIV (1951), 128; Lorenzo J. Greene, "Negroes in the Armed Forces of the United States to 1865," Negro History Bulletin, XIV (1951), 125.

11. Ibid.

12. Litwack, op. cit., p. 32.

13. Ibid., p. 33.

14. The two best books describing Lincoln's refusal to use Negro troops as well as a general discussion of Negro soldiers in the Civil War are: Dudley Taylor Cornish, The Sable Arm: Negro Troops in the Union Army, 1861-1865 (New York: Longmans, Green, 1956) and Benjamin Quarles, The Negro in the Civil War (Boston: Little, Brown, 1953).

15. Ibid.

16. Ibid.

17. Figures from Franklin, op. cit., pp. 267-92.

18. Quarles, The Negro in the Civil War, loc. cit.

19. Richard J. Stillman, U.S. Infantry (New York: Franklin Watts, Inc., 1965), pp. 299-308.

20. This includes the number of medals won in the Civil War. Data are on file in the Civil Rights Office, U.S. Department of Defense, Washington, D.C.

21. Wesley Brown, "Eleven Men of West Point," Negro History Bulletin, XIX (April, 1956), 147. Also refer to: Integration and the Negro Officer, issued by the U.S. Department of Defense (March, 1962), p. 3. Further information is found in Chapter 4, Table 6, p. 68, of this book.

22. John Hope Franklin, Reconstruction After the Civil War (Chicago: University of Chicago, 1961).

23. Frank Burt Freidal, The Splendid Little War (Boston: Little, Brown, 1958); Herchel V. Cashin, Under Fire with the Tenth U.S. Cavalry (New York: F. T. Neely, 1899).

24. C. Vann Woodward, The Strange Career of Jim Crow (New York: Oxford University Press, 1957).

25. Plessy v. Ferguson, 163 U.S. 537 (1896).

26. E. K. Thornbrough, "Brownsville," Mississippi Valley Historical Review, XLIV (December, 1957), 469.

27. Arthur S. Link, Woodrow Wilson and the Progressive Era, 1910-1917 (New York: Harper & Row, 1954).

28. Charles E. Silberman, Crisis in Black and White (New York: Random House, 1963), p. 127.

29. Robert R. Moton, Finding a Way Out (New York: Doubleday, Page & Co., 1920), p. 263.

30. W. E. B. DuBois, Crisis, XVIII, No. 1 (May, 1919), 16.

31. Ibid., p. 97.

32. Emmett Scott, The American Negro in the World War (New York, 1919), pp. 75-82.

33. W. E. B. DuBois, op. cit., p. 17.

34. Scott, op. cit., pp. 197-274.

35. W. E. B. DuBois, Crisis, XVIII, No. 1 (June, 1919), 76.

36. Pittsburgh Courier, March 19, 1960, p. 3.

37. Refer to Chapter 4, Table 11, p. 79, of this book.

38. Figures based on John Hope Franklin, From Slavery to Freedom, op. cit., pp. 444-68.

39. Colonel Charles Young, USMA archives, West Point, New York.

40. Scott, op. cit., pp. 82-92.

41. Abraham Chew, "A Biography of Colonel Charles Young," unpublished, on file in the Library of Congress, Washington, D.C., 1930.

42. John P. Davis, "The Negro in the Armed Forces of America," American Negro Reference Book (New York: Prentice-Hall, 1966), pp. 590-661.

43. Crisis (May, 1919), pp. 19-20.

44. Ibid. (June, 1919), p. 70.

45. Ibid., p. 73; see also: Arthur W. Little, From Harlem to the Rhine: The Story of New York's Colored Volunteers (New York: Covici, Friede, 1936).

46. Ibid., p. 69 and p. 79.

47. Ibid., p. 80.

48. Ulysses G. Lee, The Employment of Negro Troops in World War II (Washington, D.C.: Office of the Chief of Military History, United States Army, 1966), memo written to Secretary Henry L. Stimson on December 1, 1941, Chap. I.

49. Robert Bullard, Personalities and Reminiscences of the War (New York: Doubleday, Page & Co., 1925).

50. Lee, op. cit.

51. Armed Service Forces Manual (M5), Leadership of the Negro Soldier (Washington, D.C., October, 1944), p. 93.

NOTES TO CHAPTER 3

1. Lee Nichols, Breakthrough on the Color Front (New York: Random House, 1954), p. 36.

2. The first Negroes elected to Congress in the twentieth century were from Chicago: Oscar de Priest (1928-34), who was replaced by Arthur W. Mitchell (1934-42), who was replaced by the current incumbent William L. Dawson in 1942.

3. Jean Byers, A Study of the Negro in Military Service, unpublished manuscript available in the U.S. Army Library in the Pentagon (Washington, D.C., June, 1947), pp. 26-50 and pp. 213-38.

4. Ibid., pp. 117-63.

5. Helen Gahagan Douglas, The Negro Soldiers, Washington, D.C., Congressional Record Reprint No. 685535-15300 (February 1, 1946), pp. 20-26.

6. Byers, op. cit., p. 124.

7. Walter Francis White, A Rising Wind (New York: Doubleday, Doran & Co., 1945), p. 76.

8. Douglas, op. cit., pp. 7-13.

9. Dennis Denmark Nelson, The Integration of the Negro into the U.S. Navy (New York: Farrar, Straus & Young, 1951), pp. 24-26.

10. William Hastie, On Clipped Wings (Washington, D.C., NAACP Publication, 1943).

11. Ibid., p. 1.

12. William L. Dawson was elected from Chicago in 1942 and Adam C. Powell from New York in 1944.

13. Byers, op. cit., pp. 51-88.

14. Nelson, op. cit., pp. 76-93.

15. Ulysses G. Lee, The Employment of Negro Troops in World War II (Washington, D.C.: Office of the Chief of Military History, United States Army, 1966), memo written to Secretary Henry L. Stimson on December 1, 1941.

16. Ibid., memo of Judge William Hastie to the Secretary of War, June 13, 1942.

17. The Fahy Committee Report, Freedom to Serve (Washington, D.C.: Government Printing Office, 1950), p. 17.

18. Lee, op. cit., memo of July 2, 1942.

19. Ibid., but based upon T. W. Anderson, Come Out Fighting (New York, 1945), p. 15.

20. Byers, op. cit., pp. 164-82.

21. Douglas, op. cit., pp. 29-33.

22. U.S. Department of the Navy, A Guide to the Command of Navy Personnel (Washington, D.C., NavPers 15092, 1944).

23. Byers, op. cit., pp. 213-60; Nelson, op. cit., pp. 94-141.

24. CBS Television Program, unpublished transcript, "The Nisei: The Pride and the Shame," shown Sunday, January 3, 1965, p. 13.

25. Ibid.

26. Robert G. McCloskey, The American Supreme Court (Chicago: University of Chicago, 1960), p. 182.

27. Byers, op. cit., p. 1.

28. Witter Bynner, Take Away the Darkness (New York: Knopf, 1947), p. 48.

29. John O. Killens, And Then We Heard the Thunder (New York: Knopf, 1962).

30. Ibid.

31. Sammy Davis, Jr., and Jane and Burt Boyar, Yes I Can (New York: Farrar, Straus, 1965); excerpts quoted from "The Military Ordeal of Sammy Davis, Jr.," Ebony (December, 1965), p. 157.

32. White, op. cit., p. 155.

33. John P. Davis, "The Negro in the Armed Forces of America," American Negro Reference Book (New York, 1966), p. 110.

34. Ibid.

35. Ibid., p. 232.

36. Ibid., p. 154, p. 137, and p. 564.

37. Samuel P. Huntington, The Soldier and the State: The Theory and Politics of Civil-Military Relations (Cambridge, Mass.: Harvard, 1957), pp. 73-79; John W. Masland and Laurence I. Radway, Soldiers and Scholars: Military Education and National Policy (Princeton, N.J.: Princeton University Press, 1957), p. 506.

38. Samuel P. Huntington, "Power, Expertise, and the Military Profession," Daedalus (Fall, 1963), pp. 793-801; see also: Huntington, The Soldier and the State, op. cit., pp. 354-73.

39. U.S. War Department, "Utilization of Negro Manpower in the Postwar Army Policy," Circular 124 (Washington, D.C., April 27, 1946).

40. The New York Times, March 4, 1946, p. 25; The New York Times, March 5, 1946, p. 10.

41. Nelson, op. cit., p. 20.

42. Ibid., p. 21.

43. Ibid., p. 75.

44. Robert Albion and Robert Connery, Forrestal and the Navy (New York: Columbia University Press, 1962), p. 14.

45. The New York Times, October 30, 1947, p. 14.

46. Lawrence Dunbar Reddick, "Negro Policy of the American

Army Since World War Two," Journal of Negro History, XXXVIII
(April, 1953), 199.

47. Ibid.

48. The New York Times, March 23, 1948, p. 21.

49. Ibid.

50. The New York Times, April 1, 1948, p. 1.

51. Ibid.

52. The New York Times, April 3, 1948, p. 3.

53. Reddick, op. cit., p. 201.

54. Ibid.

55. Ibid.

56. U.S. Congress, Congressional Record, Hearings before the
Senate Armed Services Committee (March 30, 1948), p. 647.

57. The New York Times, April 3, 1948, p. 3.

58. The New York Times, June 16, 1948, p. 1.

59. Reddick, op. cit., p. 202.

60. The New York Times, May 13, 1948, p. 1.

61. The New York Times, June 27, 1948, p. 35.

62. "Segregation Thorn," Newsweek, April 12, 1948, p. 26.

63. The New York Times, June 27, 1948, p. 35.

64. Reddick, op. cit., p. 204.

65. The New York Times, June 22, 1948, p. 2.

66. Eric F. Goldman, The Crucial Decade: America, 1945–1955
(New York: Knopf, 1956), pp. 81–90.

67. The New York Times, July 27, 1948, p. 4.

68. Grant Reynolds, "A Triumph for Civil Disobedience," The Nation, August 28, 1948, pp. 228-29.

69. Ibid.

70. The New York Times, August 8, 1948, p. 51.

71. The New York Times, September 19, 1948, p. 61.

72. Huntington, The Soldier and the State, op. cit., p. 378.

73. The New York Times, April 21, 1949, p. 14; The New York Times, April 29, 1949, p. 7.

74. Nichols, op. cit., pp. 75-76.

75. Ibid., pp. 79-81.

76. The New York Times, May 12, 1948, p. 1.

77. Nichols, op. cit., p. 105; The New York Times, September 18, 1949, p. 53.

78. Defense leaders like General George Marshall had feared that with the end of the quota for Negroes, they would increase to one third of the military. See Nichols, op. cit., p. 106.

79. For figures of lower-middle-class origins of Air Force Officers as compared to Army and Navy personnel, refer to Morris Janowitz, The Professional Soldier: A Social and Political Portrait (Glencoe, Ill.: Free Press, 1960), p. 90; for the lower class's higher intolerance toward Negroes, refer to Gordon Willard Allport, The Nature of Prejudice (Cambridge, Mass.: Addison-Wesley, 1954), pp. 64-79.

80. Table 2, Chapter 4, p. 64.

81. Table 12, Chapter 4, p. 80.

82. Nichols, op. cit., p. 80.

83. The New York Times, June 8, 1949, p. 16.

84. Freedom to Serve, op. cit., as quoted in The New York Times, May 23, 1950, p. 1.

85. E. W. Kenworthy, "Taps for Jim Crow," The New York Times Magazine, June 11, 1950, p. 12.

86. Information based upon discussions with James C. Evans, Pentagon Civil Rights, Counselor, February 20, 1966.

87. Huntington, "Power, Expertise, and the Military Profession," op. cit.

88. Huntington, The Soldier and the State, op. cit., p. 429 footnote.

89. The New York Times, May 12, 1949, p. 1; The New York Times, June 8, 1949, p. 16; The New York Times, July 17, 1949, p. 1.

90. The New York Times, October 1, 1949, p. 8.

91. The New York Times, November 4, 1949, p. 51; The New York Times, January 16, 1950, p. 1; The New York Times, January 17, 1950, p. 11.

92. Ibid.

93. Nichols, op. cit., p. 107-10.

94. Project CLEAR, Utilization of Negro Manpower, Vol. III, Appendix, Operations Research Office, Johns Hopkins University, June 30, 1951.

95. Harold H. Martin, "How Do Our Negro Troops Measure Up?" Saturday Evening Post (June 16, 1951), p. 30; for Negro reaction to this article, see: "Editorial," Ebony (September, 1951), p. 96; for a Communist Negro view of colored troop participation in the Korean Conflict, refer to Benjamin J. Davis, "On the Use of Negro Troops in Wall Street's Aggression Against the Korean People," Political Affairs (October, 1950), p. 47.

96. Project CLEAR, op. cit., p. 1.

97. Richard J. Stillman, U.S. Infantry (New York: Franklin Watts, Inc., 1965), pp. 305-07.

98. U.S. Congress, Congressional Record, Vol. 98, Pt. 8, p. 10866 (September, 1950).

99. The New York Times, July 27, 1951, p. 2; The New York Times, August 2, 1951, p. 2.

100. E. Leiser, "For Negroes It's a New Army Now," Saturday Evening Post (December 13, 1952), p. 26 ff.

101. Ibid.

102. Ibid.

103. Ibid.

104. Nichols, op. cit., p. 134-42.

105. Project CLEAR, op. cit., Appendix.

NOTES TO CHAPTER 4

1. The New York Times, October 31, 1954, p. 23.

2. Ibid.

3. The New York Times, March 2, 1954, p. 6; Lee Nichols, Breakthrough on the Color Front (New York: Random House, 1954), pp. 189-200.

4. The New York Times, October 30, 1952, p. 30.

5. Ibid., p. 26.

6. The New York Times, October 5, 1956, p. 14.

7. The New York Times, October 6, 1956, p. 10.

8. "Every GI a King," Ebony (April, 1953), p. 36.

9. The New York Times, June 28, 1953, p. 41; The New York Times, December 30, 1954, p. 10.

10. David Halberstam, "The Army Looks Good to John Lawrence," The Reporter (October 3, 1957), p. 24.

11. C. C. Moskos, "Has the Army Killed Jim Crow?" Negro History Bulletin (November, 1957), p. 27.

12. The New York Times, July 3, 1953, p. 9; The New York Times, May 19, 1955, p. 13; The New York Times, March 31, 1956, p. 30; The New York Times, May 21, 1956, p. 21.

13. James Q. Wilson, "Two Negro Politicians: An Interpretation," Midwest Journal of Political Science (November, 1960), pp. 346-69. A check of Powell's and Dawson's offices, February 18, 1966, revealed that Powell maintains a full-time staff member to deal with Negro Armed Forces personnel requests (even if the soldiers are not from the Harlem district). Dawson's office has no such aide nor does it make any special effort to help Negro military men not from Chicago.

14. Anthony Lewis, Portrait of a Decade: The Second American Revolution (New York: Random House, 1964), p. ix.

15. Based on discussions with James C. Evans in the Civil Rights Office, U.S. Department of Defense, Washington, D.C., February 20, 1966, and the summer of 1965. For details on the reduction of racial tensions, see: Leo Bogart, "The Army and Its Negro Soldiers," The Reporter (December 30, 1954), p. 8; The New York Times, June 28, 1953, p. 30; The New York Times, September 8, 1954, p. 35; and Charles E. Silberman, Crisis in Black and White (New York: Random House, 1963), p. 63 footnote. For the higher frequency of racial tensions in World War II, see Jean Byers, A Study of the Negro in Military Service, unpublished manuscript available in the U.S. Army Library in the Pentagon (Washington, D.C., June, 1947), pp. 51-88; Samuel Andrew Stauffer, The American Soldier (Princeton, N.J.: Princeton University Press, 1949), chap. on Negro troops; and The New York Times, June 29, 1951, p. 24.

16. John B. Spore, "Our Negro Soldiers: Korea," The Reporter (June 22, 1952), p. 6.

17. The Fahy Committee Report, Freedom to Serve (Washington, D.C.: Government Printing Office, May, 1950), reprinted in part in The New York Times, May 22, 1950, p. 1, text of Truman's comments on p. 9.

18. Gen. Mark W. Clark, "Clark: Negro Battalions 'Weakened Battleline,'" U.S. News and World Report (May 11, 1956), pp. 54-56; The New York Times, April 28, 1956, p. 37.

19. The New York Times, April 28, 1956, p. 37.

20. The New York Times, May 6, 1956, p. 4.

21. Harold H. Martin, "How Do Our Negro Troops Measure Up?" Saturday Evening Post (June 16, 1951), p. 30 ff.

22. Brown v. the Board of Education of Topeka, 347 U.S. 483 (1954).

23. Discussion with Professor Thomas F. Pettigrew, William James Building, Harvard University, Cambridge, October, 1965.

24. John Wiant, "Integration a Fact in Services but--," Army, Navy, Air Force Register (November 28, 1959), p. 1; also refer to Negro History Bulletin (April, 1960), pp. 151-52.

25. Refer to Table 2, Chapter 4, p. 64.

26. Based upon figures available in the Civil Rights Office, U.S. Department of Defense, Washington, D.C.

27. The New York Times, January 3, 1966, p. 8.

28. Based upon figures available in the Civil Rights Office, U.S. Department of Defense, Washington, D.C.

29. Rashi Fein, "An Economic and Social Profile of the Negro American," Daedalus (Fall, 1965), p. 830.

30. Ibid., p. 824 and p. 827.

31. Morris Janowitz (ed.), The New Military: Changing Patterns of Organization (New York: Russell Sage Foundation, 1964), p. 43.

32. Ibid., p. 42.

33. Samuel P. Huntington, "Power, Expertise, and the Military Profession," Daedalus (Fall, 1963), pp. 793-801.

34. The New York Times, February 6, 1966, p. E 9.

35. Daniel Patrick Moynihan, "Employment, Income, and the Ordeal of the Negro Family," Daedalus (Fall, 1965), p. 747.

36. Ebony (January, 1966), p. 41.

37. The New York Times, January 3, 1966, p. 8.

38. Ibid.

39. For example, the Air Force Academy 1965-1966 Catalogue (p. 18) lists where its 3,200 appointments come from as follows:

100 Senators (5 appointments each)	500	
435 Representatives (5 each)	2,175	
Vice President	5	
District of Columbia	5	
Puerto Rico	6	
Canal Zone	1	
Guam, Virgin Islands, Samoa	1	
Sons of Deceased Veterans	68	
Philippines	4	
American Republics	20	
Presidential	75	(annual)
Regular Component	85	(annual)
Reserve Component	85	(annual)
Honor Military Schools	20	(annual)
Qualified Alternates	150	(annual)
Sons of Winners of the Medal of Honor	no limit	

Note: It is with the "Qualified Alternates" that the academies have a considerable degree of choice in selection, and it is here that more efforts could be made to increase Negro attendance.

40. Wesley Brown, "Eleven Men of West Point," Negro History Bulletin (April, 1956), p. 147.

41. Huntington, "Power, Expertise, and the Military Profession," op. cit.

42. Janowitz, op. cit., pp. 257-85.

43. Based upon figures available in the Civil Rights Office, U.S. Department of Defense, Washington, D.C.

44. Ibid.

45. Concept of fifteen nations' war colleges as social institutions to be advanced in a three-part article by Richard J. Stillman, "A Critical Analysis of the National War College" (to be published, Winter, 1968).

46. Brown, op. cit., p. 147; "Squadron Commander," Look (October 19, 1954), pp. 129-35; Ebony (March, 1960), pp. 27-30.

47. The President's Committee on Equal Opportunity in the Armed Forces, Equality of Treatment and Opportunity for Negro Military Personnel Within the United States, Initial Report (June 13, 1963), p. 42.

48. Ibid., p. 75.

49. Nathaniel Glazer and Daniel Patrick Moynihan, Beyond the Melting Pot: The Negroes, Puerto Ricans, Jews, Italians, and Irish of New York City (Cambridge, Mass.: M.I.T. Press, 1963), pp. 24-85.

50. Thomas F. Pettigrew, "Complexity and Change in American Racial Patterns," Daedalus (Fall, 1965), p. 980.

51. Phillip M. Hauser, "Demographic Factors in the Integration of the Negro," Daedalus (Fall, 1965), p. 853.

52. The Stackpole Publishing Company (ed.), The Officers' Guide (Harrisburg, Pa., 1963), pp. 67-105.

53. Distribution of housing benefits at military stations is based upon allocation to highest officer and NCO ranks first.

54. Harold C. Fleming, "The Federal Executive and Civil Rights: 1961-1965," Daedalus (Fall, 1965), pp. 921-48.

55. President's Committee on Equal Opportunity, op. cit., p. 70.

56. Quarters allowance for a captain with dependents is $137.00 (1968) and $110.00 (1968) for an E-5.

57. "When Negro Servicemen Bring Home White Brides," U. S. News and World Report (October 11, 1957), pp. 110-12.

58. President's Committee on Equal Opportunity, op. cit., Final Report (November, 1964), pp. 12-22.

59. _Ibid._

60. _Ibid._

61. _Ibid._

62. _Ibid._

63. _Ibid._

64. _The New York Times_, December 30, 1964, p. 28.

65. _Ibid._

66. G. I. Newton, "The Negro and the National Guard," _Phylon_ (Spring, 1962), pp. 18-28.

67. Martha Derthick, _The National Guard in Politics_ (Cambridge, Mass.: Harvard University Press, 1965).

68. _Ibid._

69. _The Federal Dollar and Nondiscrimination_ (Washington, D.C.: The Potomac Institute, March, 1965).

70. Refer to p. 119 of this book.

71. Mark S. Watson, "Guard Commands All Units to End Bias Against Negroes," _Baltimore Sun_, March 31, 1964, p. 5.

72. Newton, _op. cit._, pp. 18-28.

73. Based upon discussions with staff members of the National Guard Bureau and National Guard Association, February, 1966.

74. Statistics found in Theodore H. White, _The Making of the President, 1960_ (New York: Atheneum Publishers, 1961), p. 461.

75. Zbigniew Brzezinski and Samuel P. Huntington, _Political Power: USA/USSR_ (New York: Viking Press, 1964), p. 285.

76. _Ibid._, p. 288; for further discussion of Kennedy's civil rights approach, read Theodore C. Sorensen, _Kennedy_ (New York: Harper and Row, 1965).

77. The New York Times, October 14, 1961, p. 1.

78. President's Committee on Equal Opportunity, op. cit., Initial Report, p. 1.

79. The New York Times, January 24, 1963, p. 5.

80. Ibid.

81. President's Committee on Equal Opportunity, op. cit.

82. Ibid.

83. Ibid.

84. Refer to p. 115 of this book.

85. Based on information obtained from the Civil Rights Office, U.S. Department of Defense, Washington, D.C.

86. Ibid.

87. The New York Times, June 26, 1963, p. 1.

88. Ibid.

89. The New York Times, December 30, 1964, p. 28.

90. Based on information obtained from the Civil Rights Office, U.S. Department of Defense, Washington, D.C.

91. "The Pentagon Jumps Into the Race Fight," U.S. News and World Report (August 19, 1963), pp. 49-50; for Southern Conservative attack on McNamara, see: "Georgia Vinson Battling Pentagon," U.S. News and World Report (September 30, 1963); Army, Navy, Air Force Journal (September 21, 1963), p. 1; and The New York Times, August 1, 1963, p. 1.

92. The New York Times, July 17, 1963, p. 1; The New York Times, July 27, 1963, p. 1.

93. Based on information obtained from the Civil Rights Office, U.S. Department of Defense, Washington, D.C.

NOTES TO CHAPTER 5

1. A statement issued on a mimeographed sheet in Kirkland House, Harvard University, and available in my files on request. Bond's figures are incorrect, for the Negro draft rate is 16.3 per cent (not considerably different from their 11.9 per cent of the national population), according to The New York Times, January 3, 1966, p. 8. They are currently about 18 per cent of the Army combat forces in South Vietnam and have, over the past five years, sustained an average 18.3 per cent of the combat deaths, according to The New York Times, March 10, 1966, p. 4. Two pressures are creating this somewhat higher casualty rate: one, their imbalanced distribution among lower ranks--officers and NCO--where the higher fatalities occur (refer to Chapter 4); and two, the categories of the American draft laws which exempt students and those involved in special skills, but not working-class individuals (a role the bulk of young Negroes occupy). This situation has created dissatisfaction among many urban Negroes, and Bond's statement is a good reflection of their dissent.

2. Samuel P. Huntington, "Power, Expertise, and the Military Profession," Daedalus (Fall, 1963), pp. 793-801.

3. Ibid.

4. Mimeographed statement made at Kirkland House, Harvard University, loc. cit. ; The New York Times, January 3, 1966, p. 8; The New York Times, March 10, 1966, p. 4; and also see Chapter 4 of this book.

5. DuBois became a Communist and eventually left America for Africa where he died; Washington, a political leader at the turn of the twentieth century, monopolized the Negro movement with his philosophy and Tuskegee organization to the exclusion of more militant colored voices. Refer to Charles E. Silberman, Crisis in Black and White (New York: Random House, 1963).

6. Alexis de Tocqueville, Democracy in America, Vol. 1 (New York: Knopf, 1960), p. 373.

7. Morton Puner, "What the Armed Forces Taught Us About Integration," Coronet (June, 1959), p. 101.

8. Lee Nichols, Breakthrough on the Color Front (New York: Random House, 1954), p. 109.

BIBLIOGRAPHICAL ESSAY

BIBLIOGRAPHICAL ESSAY

For the reader who wishes to learn more about the Negro and the military, this essay is intended to point the way to the most appropriate sources. Some of the following books are out of print, but all are available at the six major collections on American Negro military history. The Schomburg Collection at the New York Public Library has valuable information on the Revolution and Civil War periods. The National Archives in Washington has good material on the Civil War and World War I eras. The Library of Congress, Widener Library at Harvard University, and the Pentagon Army Library in Washington contain good general collections of books from the Spanish-American War period to the present and have magazines and newspapers on file or microfilm. For current data, the Civil Rights Office in the U.S. Department of Defense is the best source. The offices and files of the leading Negro journals offer a wealth of material: the Chicago Defender, the Pittsburgh Courier, and Ebony Magazine. Two books by the Military Historical Section in Washington will be valuable reference sources to scholars: Major Ulysses G. Lee's The Employment of Negro Troops in World War II (Washington, D.C.: Office of the Chief of Military History, United States Army, 1966), and Martin Blumenson's study of military integration before and during Korea (to be published in 1968).

While unrelated to the Negro problem, there are several books which are important for gaining an understanding of the nature of the military organization. Samuel P. Huntington has made a brilliant study of defense structure and how it relates to American politics in his two books: The Soldier and the State: The Theory and Politics of Civil-Military Relations (Cambridge, Mass.: Harvard University Press, 1957), and The Common Defense (New York: Columbia University Press, 1961). Martha Derthick's The National Guard in Politics (Cambridge, Mass.: Harvard University Press, 1965), gives an excellent insight into the character of the National Guard. John W. Masland's and Laurence I. Radway's Soldiers and Scholars: Military Education and National Policy (Princeton, N.J.: Princeton University Press, 1957), is a necessary book for an appreciation of the system of military education. The sociological character of the men and organizational values of the Armed Forces are well explained in

Morris Janowitz's The Professional Soldier: A Social and Political
Portrait (Glencoe, Ill.: Free Press, 1960). The President's Com-
mission on Veterans Benefits, a Report (April, 1956), has data on
the effects of technological change in the military. Factual background
on American military history is contained in two quite readable books:
Walter Mills's Arms and Men: A Study in American Military History
(New York: Putnam, 1956), and ROTC Manual 145-20, American
Military History, 1607 to 1958 (Department of the Army, July, 1959).

For the broad picture of the Negro's dilemma in America,
John Hope Franklin's From Slavery to Freedom: A History of
American Negroes (2nd ed., rev.; New York: Knopf, 1956), gives
the best historical account of the relation of the Negro's African
origins to the present civil rights struggle. Charles E. Silberman's
Crisis in Black and White (New York: Random House, 1963), contains
more interpretation of Negro history. Three shorter historical sum-
maries of Negro history are Rayford W. Logan's The Negro in the
United States: A Brief History (Princeton, N.J.: D. Van Nostrand
Co., 1957), Benjamin Quarles's The Negro in the Making of America
(New York: Collier Books, 1964); and Carter G. Woodson's and
Charles H. Wesley's The Negro in Our History (10th ed., rev.;
Washington, D.C.: Associated Publishers, 1962). The father of sociological studies on the Negro is Gunnar Myrdal's The American
Dilemma (New York: Harper, 1944), but his statistics and ideas
are somewhat outdated today. Thomas F. Pettigrew's A Profile of
the American Negro (Princeton, N.J.: D. Van Nostrand, 1964), pre-
sents a more current view of psychological and sociological pressures
on the Negro. The attitudes of the middle-class colored are presented
in Edward Franklin Frazier's Black Bourgeoisie (Glencoe, Ill.: Free
Press, 1957), and the problems of the urban poor are explained in
Kenneth Bancroft Clark's Dark Ghetto: Dilemmas of Social Power
(New York: Harper & Row, 1965), and Nathaniel Glazer's and Daniel
Patrick Moynihan's Beyond the Melting Pot: The Negroes, Puerto
Ricans, Jews, Italians, and Irish of New York City (Cambridge, Mass.:
M.I.T. Press, 1963). A very fine description of Negro politics is
found in James Q. Wilson's Negro Politics: The Search for Leader-
ship (Glencoe, Ill.: Free Press, 1960), and a chapter in City Politics
(Cambridge, Mass.: Harvard University Press, 1963), by Professors
Edward C. Banfield and James Q. Wilson. For the most up-to-date
data and scholarly views on Negroes, three recent publications are
valuable reading. The Fall, 1965, and Winter, 1966, issues of
Daedalus are devoted entirely to the American Negro and have
articles by leading historians, political scientists, economists,
sociologists, and psychologists on the topic. The year 1966 saw the
publication of the American Negro Reference Book, edited by John P.

Davis, which likewise has several articles by different scholars.
Chapters 4 and 15, on Negro employment and Negroes in the Armed
Forces, are well written and contain some important material on
Negro-military relations.

As for the historical context of Negro-military relations beginning with the Revolution, the finest book both in respect to research
and writing style is The Negro in the American Revolution, by Negro
historian Benjamin A. Quarles at the University of North Carolina
(Chapel Hill, 1961). Two interesting perspectives on the subject are
by a northern abolitionist and a Negro Communist, respectively,
William Lloyd Garrison's The Loyalty and Devotion of Colored Americans in the Revolution and War of 1812 (Boston: R. F. Wallcut, 1861),
and Herbert Aptheker's The Negro in the American Revolution (New
York: International Publishers, 1940). Four short articles add dimensions to a perspective on the Negro in the Revolutionary War:
Lorenzo J. Greene's "Negroes in the Armed Forces of the United
States to 1865," in the Negro History Bulletin, XIV (1951), 125;
Lorenzo J. Greene's "Some Observations on the Black Regiment in
the American Revolution," in the Journal of Negro History, XXVII
(1942), 142; Luther Porter Jackson's "Virginia Negro Soldiers and
Seamen in the American Revolution," in the Journal of Negro His-
tory, XXVII (1942), 247; and Benjamin Quarles's "The Colonial
Militia and Negro Manpower," in Mississippi Valley Historical
Review, XLV (1959), 643.

Why the Negroes were not in the Army or Navy between the
Revolution and the Civil War, except for a few instances in the War
of 1812 and the Naval War with France, is described by four recent
excellent historical studies on Southern slavery and Northern segregation: Kenneth M. Stampp's The Peculiar Institution (New York:
Knopf, 1956); Leon F. Litwack's North of Slavery: The Negro in the
Free States, 1790-1860 (Chicago: University of Chicago Press, 1961);
Louis Filler's The Crusade Against Slavery, 1830-1960 (New York:
Harper & Row, 1960); and Stanley M. Elkins's Slavery: A Problem
in American Institutional and Intellectual Life (Chicago: University
of Chicago Press, 1959).

The two best books on the Negro in the Civil War, both
detailed but interesting reading, are Dudley Taylor Cornish's The
Sable Arm: Negro Troops in the Union Army, 1861-1865 (New York:
Longmans, Green, 1956), and Benjamin Quarles's The Negro in the
Civil War (Boston: Little, Brown, 1953). Two older but no less
important works on Negro Civil War history written by participants
are Thomas Wentworth Higginson's Army Life in a Black Regiment

(republished in New York: Collier Books, 1962), and Joseph Thomas Wilson's The Black Phalanx: A History of the Negro Soldiers of the United States in the Wars of 1775-1812, 1861-'65 (Hartford, Conn.: American Publishing Company, 1892). Robert French wrote a good biography of the commander of the Massachusetts Colored Unit, Colonel Robert G. Shaw (Boston: Merrymount Press, 1904). Three views of the Negro in the Civil War are treated by a Northern Negro abolitionist, a Negro Communist, and a Negro political leader, respectively: Fredrick Douglass's Men of Color to Arms! (Rochester, N.Y., 1863); Herbert Aptheker's To Be Free: Studies in American Negro History (New York: International Publishers, 1948); and Booker T. Washington's The Story of the Negro: The Rise of the Race from Slavery (2 vols.; New York: Doubleday, Page & Co., 1909).

What happened to the American Negro after the Civil War is explained by two historical interpretations: John Hope Franklin's Reconstruction: After the Civil War (Chicago: University of Chicago Press, 1961), and C. Vann Woodward's The Strange Career of Jim Crow (New York: Oxford University Press, 1957). Three more detailed studies of this era are Paul Herman Buck's The Road to Reunion, 1865-1900 (Boston: Little, Brown and Company, 1937); C. Vann Woodward's Reunion and Reaction: The Compromise of 1877 and the End of Reconstruction (Boston: Little, Brown and Company, 1951); and Rayford W. Logan's The Negro in American Life and Thought: The Nadir, 1877-1901 (New York: Dial Press, 1954).

Sidney Edgerton Whitman, The Troopers: An Informal History of the Plains Calvary, 1865-1890 (New York: Hastings House Publishers, 1962) offers the best picture of Negro regular troops, and three books have been written of specific units: Major Edward L. N. Glass's The History of the Tenth Cavalry, 1866-1921 (Tucson, Ariz.: Acme Printing Company, 1921); William G. Muller's The Twenty-Fourth Infantry, Past and Present (n.p., 1923); and John H. Nankivell's The History of the Twenty-Fifth Regiment, United States Infantry, 1869-1926 (Denver: The Smith-Brooks Printing Company, 1927). The first Negro graduates of West Point penned their comments about the service academy and military life in The Colored Cadet at West Point (New York: H. Lee & Co., 1878), and Negro Frontiersman (New York, 1878) by Henry O. Flipper. A further study of early Negro academy graduates is Wesley Brown's "Eleven Men of West Point," in the Negro History Bulletin (April, 1956); Brown was the first Negro graduate of Annapolis in 1949. S. W. Sewage gives a good account of Negro soldiers as Indian fighters in

"The Role of Negro Soldiers Protecting the Indian Territory," in the Journal of Negro History (1951).

Frank Burt Freidal's The Splendid Little War (Boston: Little, Brown and Company, 1958) gives a lively account of how America fought the Spanish-American War and tells what part the Ninth and Tenth Cavalry played in Roosevelt's Rough Riders. Herschel V. Cashin elaborates on this combat role in Under Fire with the Tenth U.S. Cavalry (New York: F.T. Neely, 1899). The activities of an infantry unit are described in W. T. Goode's The "Eighth Illinois" (Chicago: The Blakeley Printing Company, 1899). The two most detailed works on colored participation are Edward A. Johnson's History of Negro Soldiers in the Spanish-American War, and Other Items of Interest (Raleigh, N.C.: Capital Printing Company, 1899), and Theophilus Gould Steward's The Colored Regulars in the U.S. Army (Philadelphia: A.M.E. Book Concern, 1904).

E. L. Thornbrough's "Brownsville," in the Mississippi Valley Historical Review, XLIV (December, 1957), 469, relates the issues in a riot that began the strained Negro-military relations after the turn of the century. The Macklin Court Martial Hearings in the Senate Documents of the Sixtieth Congress, 1907-08 (Senate Report Number 155, Part 1 and Part 2), and in the Eleventh Volume of Senate Documents in the Second Session of the Fifty-ninth Congress, 1906-07, are the original source materials which offer good insights into white, Negro, and governmental attitudes toward Brownsville.

The Negro in World War I is a very involved subject which, so far, accomplished historians have not treated. One is then left with the subject treated from various perspectives. Scott's Official History of the American Negro in the World War by Emmett J. Scott (Chicago: Homewood Press, 1919) is a large tome with many facts and statistics, but Scott's interpretation of events omits many of the cruel experiences Negroes had to endure in uniform. The book reflects either how out of touch Scott was with reality or how an individual vindicates his actions after wartime. Robert R. Moton's Finding a Way Out: An Autobiography (New York: Doubleday, Page & Co., 1920) describes his speeches to Negro soldiers in Europe, having been asked to go there by President Wilson. Moton's account of what he did relates how a capable Negro could be utilized to achieve the ends of white politicians. W. Allison Sweeney, Chicago Defender war correspondent, has written a somewhat better book than Scott or Moton, History of the American Negro in the Great World War (Chicago: Cuneo-Henneberry Company, 1919), but Sweeney suffers from an enthusiasm to make more Negroes heroes

than their numbers or social position permit. The Negro writer that
came closest to reality was the Harvard history Ph.D. and editor of
Crisis, W. E. B. DuBois, whose issues of Crisis, particularly May
and June of 1919, show his concern as well as first-hand research
on the subject of the conditions of Negro troops in Europe. His publication of "Secret Information Concerning Black American Troops" in
the May, 1919, issue of Crisis gives valuable documentation of white
officer views toward Negro soldiers. One white officer who was
largely responsible for formulating Army opinion toward Negroes was
Robert Bullard, Second Army Commander (the Ninety-second was
under his command). For an understanding of Bullard's beliefs, his
book, Personalities and Reminiscences of the War (New York: Doubleday, Page & Co., 1925), is valuable, as are two of his articles:
"Minority Report," in Opportunity, III (July, 1925), 194, and "The
Negro Volunteer: Some Characteristics," in Military Service Institution of the United States, XXIX (July, 1901). General John J. Pershing,
a war leader who attempted to be fair to Negroes but was too removed
from commanding them and too pressed by wartime demands to aid
their plight, expresses his views in My Experience in the World War
(New York: Frederick A. Stokes Company, 1931). The net result of
military thinking toward the Negro because of World War I can be
found in the Army War College Study (November 12, 1936), "Use of
Negro Manpower in Time of War." What happened to the senior
Negro officer during World War I is described by Abraham Chew in
a biography of Colonel Charles Young, written on his death and
available in the Library of Congress.

     For detailed battlefield tactical movements of the Ninety-second
and Ninety-third Divisions, the American Battle Monuments Commission prepared two studies on this subject, which are available in
their Washington, D.C., office. Operations of the 369th Regiment are
found in Arthur W. Little's From Harlem to the Rhine: The Story of
New York's Colored Volunteers (New York: Covici, Friede, 1936).
The 371st Regiment has been written about in Chester D. Heywood's
Negro Combat Troops in the World War: The Story of the 371st In-
fantry (Worcester, Mass.: Commonwealth Press, 1928). Four
other books that add to the general information about Negroes in
World War I are Addie W. Hunton's and Kathryn M. Johnson's Two
Colored Women with the American Expeditionary Forces (Brooklyn,
N.Y.: Brooklyn Eagle Press, 1920); Monroe Mason's The American
Negro Soldier with the Red Hand of France (Boston: The Cornhill
Company, 1920); Charles Halston Williams's Sidelights on Negro
Soldiers (Boston: B. J. Brimmer, 1923); and William Irwin MacIntyre's
Colored Soldiers (Macon, Ga.: The J. W. Burke Company, 1923).

Information on World War II has been improved with the publication
of Major Ulysses G. Lee's The Employment of Negro Troops in World
War II (Washington, D. C.: Office of the Chief of Military History,
United States Army, 1966). Although it is not easy reading because of
its mass of details, Lee's book carefully documents the military organization's policy toward Negroes. Jean Byers' The Study of the Negro in the
Military Service (June, 1947), an unpublished document on file in the
Pentagon Army Library, presents a good general survey of Negro
soldiers in World War II, but suffers from a lack of footnotes to explain where some of the information was obtained. Sociological data
of the problems segregation caused in provoking racial tension can
be found in Samuel Andrew Stauffer's The American Soldier (2 vols.;
Princeton, N.J.: Princeton University Press, 1949); one chapter is
on Negro soldiers. Representative Helen Gahagan Douglas presented
a concise summary of Negroes in World War II in the House of Representatives, February 1, 1946, to be found in the Congressional Record,
Reprint No. 685535-15300. Three books focus on the Negro policy in
each service: Robert S. Beightler's The Negro in the Armed Forces
(1948), an unpublished thesis in the Army Pentagon Library, concen-
trates on the Army's World War II and postwar policy. Dennis D.
Nelson's The Integration of the Negro into the U.S. Navy (New York:
Farrar, Straus, and Young, 1951) offers a description of the Navy's
policies before, during, and after World War II. Charles E. Francis's
The Tuskegee Airmen: The Story of the Negro in the U.S. Air Force
(Boston: Bruce Humphries, 1956) relates the war experience and
heroism of the Negroes in the Army Air Corps.

For three contrasting viewpoints on the Negro's role in
World War II, see the following: The Army War College Report
(May, 1942) on file in the Army Historical Section, Washington, D.C.,
relates the thinking of senior military officers and shows how deeply
they were influenced by the World War I experience. Walter Francis
White's A Rising Wind (Garden City, N.Y.: Doubleday, Doran and
Company, Inc., 1945) and A Man Called White: The Autobiography
of Walter White (New York: Viking Press, 1948) express the views
of the NAACP Secretary toward the military organization's wartime
policy. Seymour J. Schoenfeld's The Negro in the Armed Forces,
His Value and Status, Past, Present, and Potential (Washington, D.C.:
The Associated Publishers, 1945) is a good example of the newly
expressed ideological commitment many whites came to have toward
Negro equality at home after fighting totalitarianism abroad.

Several good magazine articles present further insight into
the World War II period: Charles Dollard's and Donald Young's
"The Negro in the Armed Forces," Survey Graphic (January, 1947);

E. Franklin Frazier's "Ethnic Minority Groups in Wartime," American Journal of Sociology (November, 1942); Earl Brown's "The American Negro and the War," Harper's (April, 1942); "The Negro's War," Fortune (June, 1942); Amidon Beulah's "Negroes and Defense," Survey Graphic (June, 1941); and John A. Davis's "The Negro Outlook Today," Survey Graphic (November, 1942). William Hastie's On Clipped Wings, an NAACP pamphlet (1943), is important reading for an understanding of Negro problems in the Army Air Corps. Two articles give some information on Negroes in the Navy: L. D. Reddick's "The Negro in the U. S. Navy," Journal of Negro History (April, 1947), and F. K. Paul's "Yeoman First Class: Negro," Survey Graphic (August, 1947). Several magazine articles focus on the colored dilemma in the Army: R. F. Cocklin's "Report on the Negro Soldier," Infantry Journal (December, 1946); W. Welliver's "Report on the Negro Soldier," Harper's (April, 1946); and Walter White's "What the Negro Thinks of the Army," Annals of the American Academy of Political Science (September, 1942).

To sense the shift in Negro attitudes after World War II, one might look at two books by Negroes before the War and two written afterward. Booker T. Washington's Up from Slavery and James Weldon Johnson's Autobiography of an Ex-Colored Man (reprinted in New York, 1965) are both good indications of views, temperament, and actions of two Negro leaders at the turn of the century. James Baldwin's The Fire Next Time (New York: The Dial Press, 1963) or Richard Wright's Black Boy (10th ed. ; New York: The World Publishing Company, 1945) represent the new spirit of postwar middle-class Negro dissent. Witter Bynner's Take Away the Darkness (New York: Knopf, 1947); John Oliver Killens's And Then We Heard the Thunder (New York: Knopf, 1963); and Sammy Davis, Jr.'s Yes I Can (New York: Farrar, Straus, 1965) exemplify Negro reactions to World War II experiences. In the book of twenty-five war stories of Dorothy Sterling's I Have Seen War (New York: Hill and Wang, 1960), one story is entitled "In a Strange Country" and is about a Negro soldier's World War II experience in England. In Alain Albert's The Crossing (New York: G. Braziller, 1964), there is a good selection about a Negro from Mississippi and his reaction to combat in Korea.

For a broad view of what was happening in America in the postwar decade, Princeton historian Eric F. Goldman's The Crucial Decade: America, 1945-1955 (New York: Knopf, 1956) offers an adequate description. Harry S. Truman's Memoirs: Years of Trial and Hope (New York: Doubleday & Co. , 1956) gives the story of an important participant in military integration. Samuel P. Huntington's "Power, Expertise, and the Military Profession,"

Daedalus (Fall, 1963), briefly explains the transformation of the defense establishment since World War II, and Robert G. Albion's and Robert H. Connery's Forrestal and the Navy (New York: Columbia University Press, 1962) indicates the impact of Secretary Forrestal on the Navy Department during and after World War II.

Four government documents are necessary for understanding changing government policies toward uniformed Negroes in the immediate postwar period: Utilization of Negro Manpower in the Postwar Army Policy (The Gillem Board Report), War Department Circular 124, Washington, D. C.; To Secure These Rights, President Truman's Committee on Civil Rights, report issued in 1947; Executive Order 9981 (Truman's Armed Forces Equality Order), issued July 26, 1948; and the Fahy Committee Report, Freedom to Serve, Government Printing Office, May, 1950.

The best study of Negro politics during this period as it relates to the military establishment is L. D. Reddick's "The Negro Policy of the American Army Since World War II," Journal of Negro History (April, 1952). Several short magazine stories capture part of the spirit of their dissent: "The Segregation Thorn," Newsweek (April 12, 1948); "Face the Music," Time (April 12, 1948); "Randolph Announces Disobedience Tactics," The New York Times, June 27, 1948; and "Triumph for Civil Disobedience," The Nation (August 28, 1948).

So far, Lee Nichols's Breakthrough on the Color Front (New York: Random House, 1954) offers the only existing explanation of administrative politics immediately after the War within the Defense Department concerning the integration of Negroes. His work, however, lacks scholarship, and our understanding of this important subject will be greatly improved when Martin Blumenson's book is finished and is published by the Defense Historical Section in 1968. Several short news articles give glimpses of what was happening inside the Pentagon: "General on Negroes," Newsweek (September 30, 1946);"Hanson Baldwin on Bradley's Views," The New York Times, August 8, 1948; "Secretary of Defense Johnson's Order," The New York Times, April 21, 1949; "First Step," Time (May 23, 1949); "Integration at Lockbourne," The New York Times, September 18, 1949; "Gordon Gray's Order," The New York Times, January 17, 1950; "The Fahy Report," The New York Times, May 23, 1950; "Taps for Jim Crow," The New York Times Magazine, June 11, 1950.

The weakness of segregated units in Korean combat is pointed out in: Project CLEAR, Utilization of Negro Manpower, three volumes, Operations Research Office at Johns Hopkins University (June 30, 1951); Roy E. Appleman's U.S. Army in the Korean War (Washington, D.C.: Office of the Chief of Military History, 1961); and Harold Martin's "How Do Our Negro Troops Measure Up," Saturday Evening Post (June 16, 1951). Individual heroics of certain Negro soldiers in the War have been written about in the Congressional Record, Vol. XCIV, Part 8 (September, 1950), p. 10866, and in Richard J. Stillman's U.S. Infantry (New York: Franklin Watts, Inc., 1965), which has a chapter on the Twenty-fourth Infantry. For what happened immediately after integrating the Twenty-fourth, see John B. Spore's "Our Negro Soldiers: Korea," The Reporter (June 22, 1952), and Ernest Leiser's "For Negroes It's a New Army Now," Saturday Evening Post (December 13, 1952).

The effects of military integration upon the Negroes in uniform and on military organization are described in the following: David Habersham's "Army Looks Good to John Lawrence," The Reporter (October 3, 1957); C. C. Moskos's "Has the Army Killed Jim Crow?" Negro History Bulletin (November, 1957); Leo Bogart's "The Army and its Negro Soldiers," The Reporter (December 30, 1954); "Does Integration Work in the Armed Forces," U.S. News and World Report (May 11, 1956); "Integration a Fact in the Services but...," Army, Navy, Air Force Register (November 28, 1959); Morton Puner's "What the Armed Forces Taught Us About Integration," Coronet (June, 1960); P. B. Foreman's "Implications of Project CLEAR," Phylon (September, 1955); "Every GI a King," Ebony (April, 1953); and J. C. Evans's and D. A. Lane's "Integration in the Armed Services," Annals of the American Academy of Social Sciences (March, 1956).

The effect of integration on the political candidates is described by the Presidential candidates' election statements on October 30, 1952, and on October 5, 1956, in The New York Times. The reaction of Negro organizations to Army policies is described in The New York Times, December 30, 1954.

Negro problems in America since Korea are generally described by Anthony Lewis's Portrait of a Decade: The Second American Revolution (New York: Random House, 1964), and in a chapter on Negroes in Theodore H. White's The Making of the President, 1960 (New York: Atheneum Publishers, 1961). President Kennedy's specific reactions to racial questions are clarified in Theodore Sorensen's Kennedy (New York: Harper & Row, 1965) and in

Zbigniew Brzezinski's and Samuel P. Huntington's <u>Political Power:</u> <u>USA/USSR</u> (New York: Viking Press, 1964). A good cross-section of current Negro leaders' views on race problems is found in the August, 1965, issue of <u>Ebony</u> magazine, which is devoted entirely to "The White Problem in America." In the realm of military problems, the latest views on problems in Armed Forces organization are expressed in <u>The New Military: Changing Patterns of Organiza-</u> <u>tion,</u> edited by Morris Janowitz (New York: Russell Sage Foundation, 1964), and Richard J. Stillman's "Pentagon Whiz Kids," <u>Proceedings,</u> Naval Institute (April, 1966).

The best treatment of current Negro problems in the Armed Forces was the Gesell Report, entitled <u>Equality of Treatment and</u> <u>Opportunity for Negro Military Personnel.</u> Its initial report was issued June 13, 1963, and its final report came in November, 1964. The sections on officer distribution and off-post segregation in the first report are especially interesting. How Secretary of Defense McNamara and his critics responded to the Gesell Report is described in "Pentagon Jumps Into Race Fight," <u>U.S. News and World</u> <u>Report</u> (August 19, 1963), and in the same magazine, "Georgia's Vinson Battling Pentagon" (September 30, 1963).

Several good articles treating problems in the National Guard are I. G. Newton's "The Negro and the National Guard," <u>Phylon</u> (Spring, 1962); Mark S. Watson's "Guard Commands All Units to End Bias," <u>Baltimore Sun,</u> March 31, 1964; "Guard's Integration Progress," <u>National Guardsman</u> (February, 1965); "Guard Given Tighter Rules Against Bias," <u>Armed Forces Times,</u> March 24, 1965; and "Token Integration of the Guard," <u>The New</u> <u>York Times,</u> December 30, 1964. For a layman's understanding of how Title VI could be applied to federally assisted programs like the National Guard, the Potomac Institute, Washington, D.C., issued <u>A Guide to Community Action Under Title VI</u> (March, 1965).

Negro participation in the War in South Vietnam is discussed in three articles: "Only One Color," <u>Newsweek</u> (December 6, 1965); "Negro Draft Ratio Exceeds Whites," <u>The New York Times,</u> January 3, 1966; and "Negro Death Rate in Vietnam Exceeds Whites," <u>The New York Times,</u> March 10, 1966.

A pictorial summary of Negroes in the military from the Revolution to the present was shown on CBS Television, April 3, 1966, on Walter Cronkite's <u>The Twentieth Century.</u>

ABOUT THE AUTHOR

Richard J. Stillman II, until recently a member of the faculty at Nkumbi International College in Zambia, Africa, has had considerable experience in dealing with racial problems. He has been a member of the Civil Rights Section of the U.S. Defense Department in Washington and has served as an assistant to the City Manager of Weathersfield, Connecticut. As the son of a colonel in the U.S. Army, Mr. Stillman has lived at numerous military bases in the United States and Europe and has observed firsthand the integration of the Negro in the U.S. Armed Forces. He also has written several monographs on the subject.

Mr. Stillman was graduated from Harvard University.